THE KEEPER OF MEMORY

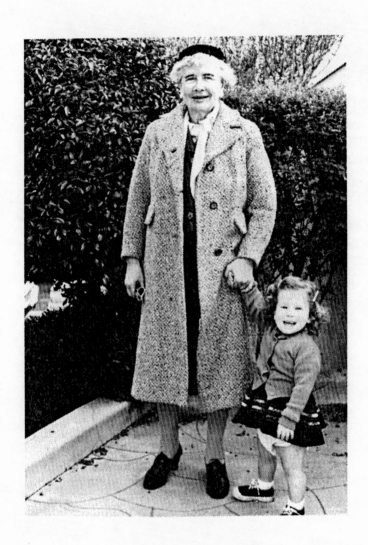

A MEMOIR BY
IRENE RETI

Printed in the United States of America by Lightning Source Printers. Distributed to the trade by Ingram Book Company 1-800-937-8000 and direct from HerBooks. Individuals may also order copies for $12.95 plus $3.00 postage direct from HerBooks.

ISBN: 0-939821-40-0

ACKNOWLEDGEMENTS

I am blessed with a large circle of friends and colleagues, many of them writers, who read and edited successive drafts of this memoir, and helped me through this journey in myriad ways. I truly could not have done it without them. I'm going to do this alphabetically because I could never figure out who to thank first! Thanks to Gloria Anzaldúa, my housemate and comadre in writing; to Judith Barrington for her book on writing the memoir, and her class on memoir writing at Flight of the Mind; to Abby Bogomolny for years of co-conspiratorship in writing and publishing; to Julia Chapin for editing advice, and especially for the week we spent writing and savoring piñon tortillas in Taos, New Mexico.

To Valerie Jean Chase, who always believed there were parallels between Indians and Jews and who supported my writing in the years we were partnered; to De Clarke, whose artistic companionship and best friendship is precious; to Esther Ehrlich for astute, meticulous, and challenging editorial consultation, and intimate friendship; to Jeanne Mayer Freebody, my sister in struggling with secrets, for passionate and critical feedback; to Carolyn Gage, for her astute wisdom; to Hannah Good, for dog walks and long talks about being JLDHS "daughters."

To Lori Green, my spiritual and psychological guide through the most difficult and transformative emotional landscapes.

To my lover and partner in life, Lori Klein, whose gifts of love, intellect, and emotional courage have been essential companions and catalysts in my personal and spiritual journey.

To Kathy Miriam, whose introspective and brilliant mind greatly benefitted this manuscript; to Amy Pine, for invaluable therapeutic work; to Susan Reddington, who faithfully encouraged me from the beginning; to Debbie Rifkin, for loving me through both the emotional and artistic challenges of this work; to Ellen Setteducati for her perceptive edits and for a delightful week writing in Missoula, Montana coffeehouses.

To Bettianne Shoney Sien, for excellent advice and companionship in so many things; to Leslie Smith, for editing advice and for being my true sister; to Ellen Farmer, Elise Ficarra, D'vora Tirschwell and Deborah Turner for editorial and personal support; to Sheri Whitt, who in a writing group years ago said, "I think that's the beginning of a book." To Barbara Wilson, for absolutely excellent editing; and to Irene Zahava, for her in-depth and heartfelt editorial assistance with draft one so many years ago.

To the members of the Whoo Has Writing Group: Sarah Rabkin, Ellen Farmer, Carol Howard, Arlyn Osborne, Robin Drury, Yael Lachman and Jude Todd, for a singular and spectacular blend of criticism and support.

Deep appreciation to the members of Jewish Lesbian Daughters of Holocaust Survivors (JLDHS), who are my "tribe," and to the members of the Kindertransport Association of America (KTA) for dedicated work on behalf of Kinder and KT2; to Helen Epstein, Helen Fremont, Alan Kaufman, and Joseph Skibell, and all the other writers of the Second Generation, for their courage and inspiration.

Special thanks also to Ilana Eden, Thea Eden, Laura Binah Feldman, Julia Graham, Rob Guillen, Jacquelyn Marie, Lesléa Newman, Tina Silverstein, Mary Stoddard, Aaron Chaim Parker, Rod Parker, Ruth Parker, and Kay Wilder. Finally, to my mother, my father, and my brother for understanding why I needed to write this book, and their courage in receiving it.

Blessings to all my chevre in Chadeish Yameinu, the Santa Cruz Jewish Renewal Havurah, for helping me find a spiritual home in Judaism. And special thanks to Rabbi Léah Novick, who has brought nature and women back to Judaism.

Finally, I want to acknowledge Cottages at Hedgebrook for the residency on Whidbey Island where I began this book, and Norcroft Writing Retreat for Women, on the North Shore of Lake Superior. These writing colonies were essential places where I could both hear my voice, and find the time to write this story. They are a gift to women writers.

Dedicated to my grandmother,
Margit Grunbaum Reti, October 29, 1900—January 6,
1997;

the children of the Holocaust—
those who survived and those who did not;

and the children of Holocaust Survivors.

CONTENTS

INTRODUCTION

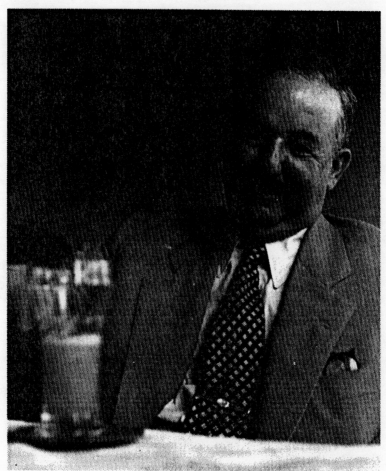

Granapu about 1970

PACIFIC VIEW CEMETERY, NEWPORT BEACH, CALIFORNIA
APRIL 1978

I wore my mother's white sandals and black dress for my grandfather's funeral. The hill we climbed at that cemetery seemed to go on forever. Grass scratched the tops of my feet which chafed against cheap, sharp buckles. My plump belly strained against the belt of the dress and my red curls frizzed in the hot wind. Why did I even come to the funeral? I never really knew my Granapu Sandor. He barely spoke English.

Rough Hungarian words tore across the cemetery lawn, guttural words, like ragged moths that swirled in the heat and died on the California soil. They were Ernie's words, and Margit's. They walked just ahead of me—my father, Ernie, tall in his black suit and my tiny Grananyu Margit in her heavy dress. His arm was linked through hers. They bent their heads close to talk.

I could smell the sea not far below us. That salty smell mixed with the scent of fertilizer and herbicides in the grass under my feet. I kicked a clump of grass. So Granapu Sandor was dead? He was an old man who could not even remember his own name. He hated people, Sandor did, claimed no one was as clever as he was. I remembered him arguing with my father throughout my whole childhood. The phone would ring, and then they'd be yelling in Hungarian, fighting long distance from New York to Los Angeles about what my father should be doing with his life. I sighed as I climbed the cemetery hill. I remembered the closed bedroom door after those phone conversations, and my father behind that door. I wanted to knock, but was afraid.

I climbed the hill and thought about my grandfather's withered legs. My grandmother had fed him with a spoon, as he sat in a plaid upholstered wheelchair that everyone pretended wasn't a wheelchair. When he had to pee my grandmother supported him. He clutched her arm, incoherent Hungarian syllables erupting from beneath his gray mustache, his tiny steps grinding into the Persian rug. My father had told me about the time Grananyu washed Granapu in the bathtub and his arms flailed out of control, hitting the hot water knob and burning his skin. Grananyu thought it was her fault, but who could wash an old man who no longer knew who he was—a man who had always been angry, even in his youth? I didn't want to remember Sandor that way—with useless legs and incoherent guttural angst—but at 17 what else did I know about this scary Hungarian man?

Finally we reached the top of the hill. I stood between my father and my brother Jeffrey, facing Granapu Sandor's grave. My father retreated inside his dark suit. His arm was still linked through his mother's.

Another man in a gray suit handed my brother something small, silky, round, and golden-colored. My brother twirled it in his hands, confused. The man commanded, "Put it on." It was a hat. I almost laughed at Jeffrey in that little hat, a mushroom growing on his black hair, but he caught my look. He frowned. I looked at my father. He had a little round hat on his head too. Suddenly, I remembered the book we were reading in my high school

English class, Chaim Potok's *The Chosen*. Could those hats be yarmulkes?

Below us lay the grave. I wondered if Granapu was really in that dark box the cemetery workers were lowering into the hole. Maybe they would slip, the box would drop onto its side and open, and Granapu would jump out yelling in Hungarian.

The box did not open. It sat there as distant as Europe seemed to me then. The man in the gray suit walked over to the grave, turned to face our family, and chanted in a solemn and melodic language I couldn't understand. It wasn't Hungarian. He only spoke for a few moments. I guessed it was some kind of prayer. Then it seemed there was nothing left to say. The workers began shoveling dirt into Granapu's grave.

I turned to follow Jeffrey down the hill back to the car, but something made me stop. I looked back. My grandmother stood by the grave alone, saying goodbye to her husband of fifty years. She looked smaller, old. Perhaps she did not want me to see her this way? I started walking. I spotted my father walking by himself way ahead of me; head drooping, he shuffled as if he didn't want to leave, didn't know where to go, now that his father was dead. Should I catch up with my father, hold his arm, comfort him? What if I touched his arm and he got mad? What if he hugged me and started crying? Would I cry then? Would I start crying and never be able to stop?

I didn't touch my father's arm that day, or wait for my grandmother to start down the hill. I walked by myself, like everyone else in the family, across the lawn, past the stucco cemetery office, to the hot asphalt parking lot. I opened the heavy door of my father's Buick, and got in the back seat next to Jeffrey. We waited in silence for my grandmother.

My father and grandmother did not speak during the slow drive along the ocean. I remember watching a sick-looking seal dive off a rock into the surf. The hills were brown. A smudge of brown smog hung over the sea.

A guard waved the car through the gates of LeisureWest after my father flashed his special visitor's pass. We parked in front of my grandparents' condo. Now it was just my grandmother's condo. Thousands of old people live in LeisureWest, in identical stucco condominiums with red tile roofs, on identical streets—Avenida Sevilla, Via Bonita, Vista Del Mar. Thousands of people with white hair. My red hair stuck out there like the flames that consumed the California hills each summer. Whenever I visited LeisureWest complete strangers marched up and tugged at my curls as if they were some kind of miracle.

My father helped his mother out of the car. "Watch your head," he warned. They made their way arm in arm down the concrete path towards the front door. I followed, my sandals clicking on the pavement.

Grananyu's living room was packed with people I had never seen before. Some came up and asked me how school was going, how had I gotten so big, did I have a boyfriend yet? I fled into a hallway and stood in front of a wall of my grandmother's paintings. Still lifes, landscapes, and portraits mingled in a river of blue, orange, and purple. I tried to breathe in the colors, my grandmother's vision. The paintings of tumultuous seas, ragged peaks, and piles of fruit added to the cacophony of the crowded apartment.

Jewish. My father is Jewish. My mother is Jewish. *I am Jewish.* I remember trying the phrases out silently. The words scratched the inside of my head. My eyes teared and my temples hurt as if lined with hundreds of tiny rubber bands, all stretching towards their breaking point. I looked down at my sandals where the buckles cut into my feet.

I had so little Jewish context in my life. Despite growing up in Hollywood, in Los Angeles, I wouldn't have recognized the language as Aramaic, the hats my brother and father wore as yarmulkes, the prayer as the Kaddish, if I had not been in the middle of reading *The Chosen* in my high school English class. I began Potok's book a non-Jew, and finished it forever altered. I was now a Jew.

Somewhere in Orange County, California there is a cemetery on a grassy hill. Wind blows dusk in from the warm sea. Granapu Sandor rests in southern California clay, near the freeway. My brother wears the small round hat, the yarmulke he never has worn before. I wear my family's amnesia like a moth-eaten *tallit*. The Kaddish falls over me. The *tallit* slips, and my family's history is revealed in the ancient words.

THE QUILTER

It's twenty years after that funeral and I would like to tell you I have it all figured out, that I am no longer the shy girl I was at age seventeen, afraid even of her own tears. I would like to construct for you a smooth narrative of my parents' lives during the Holocaust, a genealogy of destruction and survival. No such narrative exists. What remains are fragments of memory, puzzle pieces, snapshots. A funeral. A yarmulke. A girl scared to cross the street. Doilies. A Jewish prayer book written in Hungarian.

My family's story is complex, filled with choices I am still seeking to understand. Unlike many friends raised knowing they were Jewish, I was given no tools by my family for dealing with anti-semitism. I have a Jewish family that will never celebrate the cycle of holidays with me, give me any sense of pride, any reason to celebrate my heritage at all. Am I the terrible daughter, the daughter who tells family secrets, who will expose all of us? Even my brother has told me he is afraid someday my writing will put the entire family in danger.

Perhaps my red hair and blue eyes insulate me from the anti-semitism my darker, more Semitic-looking parents and brother experience in the world. It seems no accident that it is easier for me, the daughter who can pass as Irish, to claim my Jewishness, and to write this story. Recently I cut my hair short for the first time. Without my mane of curls, I am told my strong features are much more obvious. Now I look both more lesbian and more Jewish. I like this. At the same time I feel exposed.

My parents are both child refugees of the Holocaust. Should I use the word: survivor? The word survivor is often used to refer to those people who survived the concentration camps. My parents were spared this experience. Yet their childhoods were irrevocably marked by the Holocaust. They absorbed the fear of those years in their deepest and oldest selves. The paths of their lives were profoundly altered by those historical events. Were it not for the Holocaust my mother would probably have grown up a middle-class German girl, daughter of a toy manufacturer and a newspaper librarian. My father would have grown up in cosmopolitan Budapest, the son of a civil engineer and doctor. My parents would never have met and I would not be writing this.

As I set out to tell this story, I also struggled with questions of form. What genre should I choose? The first six drafts of this book were "fiction." Desiring to share this story, but also to protect my parents, I attempted to write a novel that would speak the truth of my family's history but still give them the protection of a fictional narrative. The results were unsatisfactory; the novel was too autobiographical to work as fiction. My editors and friends urged me to fictionalize the characters more, but I resisted, insisting that I wanted to document the factual trajectory of my family's history. I have compromised by changing the names of my parents, my brother, and some other members of my family.

Traversing the territory between fiction and truth, between history and memory, between poetry and persuasion, I watched these letters blur on my screen, almost palpably shaping themselves into this manuscript. It was as if the letters themselves were ghosts of ancestors past, possessing me, this California daughter, small fingers on this keyboard, praying for guidance. These were magical times when I felt as if my ancestors were helping me, rolling my fingers across the track ball on my computer, saying: "Cut this. Move this section. Yes, that's right—there."

There were other times, far too many of them, when fear made me avoid the writing completely. I debated about where to begin this narrative. Should I open with my grandfather Sandor who was buried thousands of miles from his native Hungary and wanted nothing to do with being Jewish? Or should I begin with my mother who was born in Nuremberg, Germany in 1927, and was six years old in 1933, when Hitler came to power? My mother came to the United States at age 13, but tells people, when asked, that she is from Boston. "It's true," she tells me. "They didn't ask where I was born, just where I am from. And my life began in Boston." Perhaps I should begin this book with my father, born in Budapest, Hungary in 1930, who calls himself *Földönfuto*— one who wanders this earth. Or I could start with my grandmother, my Grananyu Margit, born in 1900 in Budapest, who lost her brother to the camps, her favorite uncle to suicide when the Nazis invaded the Hungarian countryside.

"Just begin somewhere," the members of my writing group tried to reassure me. "Your book is a quilt of stories. Just concentrate on making more squares. You'll know how to piece them together." In the end it was true. What was important was not order, a linear chronology of characters and events, but a quilt or mosaic composed of fragments. For fragments are all that I really have anyway, these shards of memory sifted through my own perceptions of truth. I am the one in my family who has chosen to remember this history. Perhaps it has chosen me? I don't know. I am simply the writer arranging and re-arranging these puzzle pieces into endless patterns.

I agonized over my decision to break the familial silence about our Jewish heritage. Was this decision ethical? Was this my choice to make? I am writing about my own life, how it has been deeply affected by the Holocaust and my parents' choice to suppress their Jewishness and assimilate. Yet in this decision I am also exposing my family. I have attempted to write with deep compassion for and understanding of the complexity of my parents' choices. I have told everyone in my family what this memoir is about. Still, I feel protective of them. Is this memoir a betrayal or a gift? Perhaps my parents want me to tell the truth. Am I the missing piece, the glue for these fragmented lives? Am I my mother's missing childhood, the recorder of my father's lonely wanderings? Am I the speaker of secrets, of dreams? Am I a whisper? Am I the memorial candle, the menorah in the window, the breaker of unbearable silence at the dinner table, the one who longs for wholeness, the quilter, the one who picks up the pieces?

In the end, I decided to begin with myself. For really, this memoir is my story, a story of my quest for memory; my quest for Jewish identity and spirituality amidst the broken landscape of the Holocaust; my quest for dancing and joy and renewal amidst grief and the pressing numbness of amnesia. And so it begins in a city on the edge of the Pacific, where so many people have sought to create a new life for themselves, and turned their backs on the past.

I.

THE PAST WAS NOT A DANGER HERE:

LOS ANGELES, 1961-1978

"I am no longer a refugee because I have severed all links with the past, and have started a completely new life."

—Karen Gershon

"The past was not a danger here."

—Gary Holthaus

There was a brick house in Hollywood. I was a bright-haired child living on the second floor in a room with a narrow balcony. The balcony had green Astroturf. Its brown railings made my hands smell metallic. I leaned over the railing, and stared down to the concrete patio, and below that to the lawn fringed by ivy where my brother and I played tetherball. I lost my gold charm bracelet in that ivy when I was ten and looked for it until I was fifteen when we left that house, after the divorce.

There was a brick house in Hollywood. A brick house in the land of earthquakes. We lived there as if brick could not crumble, as if there could be no earthquakes. My father was a civil engineer who specialized in earthquake engineering, but we lived in a house of unreinforced masonry. We lived as if my parents' past had been firm, logical, ordered like bricks into a stately home. We lived as if my parents had never been refugees, as if there had never been a Holocaust. We lived as if my mother had not fled Germany at age eleven and walled the memories of her childhood behind bricks. We lived as if my father had not wandered with his parents from Hungary, to Russia, to Turkey, to Venezuela, to Boston, to California. We lived a West Coast Hollywood dream.

Yet my mother rose some mornings and in her quilted orange bathrobe told me dreams of a house in Nuremberg, a tall house where she wandered from room to room, searching for something.

And in that kitchen where I gagged on soft-boiled eggs, I watched my parents' marriage crumble, the tension split the walls, the rolled up newspaper logs we substituted for real firewood stink, smolder in the fireplace, my brother's wet brown eyelashes, my brother's open child heart close. I felt my own heart closing, too.

There were earthquakes by then, real ones, that cracked the dawn sky, sparked power lines, and sloshed the neighbors' pool toward us, as we stood, our small family, stranded on the street. "Brick houses either stand or they fall," my father always said. In other words, they have no flexibility, and when my mother chose to be free, to ride the second wave of feminism, which lifted her above the brick walls of this constricting marriage and showed her a life of consciousness-raising groups, liberated sex, and heady feminist activism—we fell. My father's dream, his foundation shattered. He met a woman and moved to her mobile home in the San Fernando Valley, while my mother, my brother and I relocated to a small yellow house on a tree-lined street in Glendale. I rode the momentum of feminism with my mother, eventually becoming an outspoken feminist lesbian writer.

I remember how the bricks smelled, hot and dusty. I would sometimes grind at one with a stick, rub the red dust into my hands. And I am haunted by another memory: I am fourteen years old. The whole family is in the den watching the made-for-TV film, *Holocaust*. A commercial comes on for Ivory soap. My mother is crying in the kitchen. She won't come back.

I was a little girl afraid of the shadow of the cuckoo clock on my bedroom wall, afraid of the plastic bird that popped out every hour after a dreadful rattling of springs. What was I so afraid of? Did I, at some level, know it was not normal to grow up in a house filled with cuckoo clocks? Were the elaborate clocks and the thick shadows they cast on dull white walls symbols of my parents' European past, a past I did not understand then, but somehow sensed and projected onto the clocks and the voice of that tiny white bird that cuckooed in the night?

What was normal were sunny yellow clocks with round open faces a child could read, not carved houses with trapped birds and heavy metal pine cone pendulums that swung on long rusty chains. What was normal were dependable electric clocks, not clocks with a little door on the back that my father had to pry open every few days and reach inside with a long key to wind.

Was it time I was afraid of as a child, time embodied in the cuckoo clock? Did I know that my parents were running from the memory of another time, but somehow the cuckoo clock, a remnant of Europe, had impaled itself on the walls of this California house, opening its mouth every hour to cry of the past?

Was it the bird I identified with, the small white bird trapped in its ornate house, destined to escape only once an hour, to come out of the little door and peek at me, terrified in my bed in the corner?

It was the moment before the cuckoo appeared that terrified me, the creaking and tensing of springs, the portent of the door opening and the cuckoo emerging. That creaking of springs would always wake me just before the cuckoo's cry would fill the bedroom.

Or was it the shadows that frightened me, the long shadows, that whispered secrets about my parents' childhoods in Nazi Europe and their near escapes from death, the shadows that spread through the house like wraiths, ghosts rousing us from our safe beds, deporting us East to that continent, away from the West, California, the land of safety. But, how could I have known about those shadows then, known what was not spoken, what only laced the air, filled the spacious rooms of that brick house, through which the cuckoo clock's insistent voice called its message?

Finally I refused to live with the cuckoo anymore. I got a digital alarm clock. The cuckoo went to live in the kitchen next to the table. When I was fourteen, my parents were fighting at breakfast one day right before the divorce. My father ripped the cuckoo clock off the wall, hurled it at the floor. It shattered: branches, pine cones, and peaked roof scattering across the beige linoleum, the little white bird coming to rest right on my tennis shoe. "Get it off me!" I screamed at my mother, but she left the room and my silent father came to pick up the pieces, to try to glue them back together.

This is a story about fear.

I was afraid of the lamp next to my bed. I was afraid to go anywhere without my mother. When I was in first grade my teacher sent a note home which read, "Irene needs to develop more confidence. Send her to the store to buy a loaf of bread." My mother took suggestions from teachers seriously. I remember begging her not to send me, whimpering as I started down the street clutching my quarter.

My mother was afraid of the freeway. She would drive the wide Los Angeles boulevards for hours, in search of deals on peaches or apricots, the hot smoggy air enveloping the interior of our light green AMC station wagon. It was the speed of the freeways that frightened her, the on-ramps, and how you had to merge into the traffic. My mother's worst fear was that she would somehow end up on one of those freeway on-ramps by mistake and lose control, be unable to avoid getting on the freeway. This only happened once in my memory. She panicked as we raced up the on-ramp, wailed, "I'm getting on the freeway!" My brother and I cowered in our seats, alarmed and helpless in the face of our mother's terror. Somehow she managed to get on the freeway and back off again, an exit later.

For my refugee parents, who desired so fervently to escape fear, to construct and then embrace their new lives as middle-class white Americans, perhaps there was no more perfect place to relocate than Hollywood.

In Hollywood, everyone believed in indoor/outdoor living, more than they believed in God. A barbecue was a necessity in southern California, essential for entertaining.

The only challenge was that my parents had fallen in love with an East-Coast style, two-story brick house with a backyard that sloped down a hill in terraces. Perhaps this love represented the vestiges of European taste, or some buried refusal to completely assimilate into the land of tract houses and swimming pools. In any case, this lack of a sliding glass door and a patio was not a problem for my father, who always had a flair for mechanical invention. He rigged up a trolley system on a clothesline that extended from the kitchen window to the lawn, a few hundred feet below the house. On command from my father, who waited by the coals, my mother would release a cardboard box packed with marinated steak, salt, pepper, paper plates and corn on the cob. The box descended into my father's waiting hands. This worked fine, even impressed a number of engineers and their wives, who would watch the box descend, open-mouthed. It was much more interesting than a sliding glass door and a patio.

I ate European style, like my father, cutting my food up a little piece at a time and then savoring it. My parents argued at the dinner table. Should the children eat American style or European style? My mother subdivided her pork chops into little pieces, before putting down the knife and eating them. My father kept the knife in his hand and ate one piece at a time, still holding on to the knife. My father said that the American way the food got cold. What does this way of eating say about America? Why do I eat like my father instead of my mother?

Child of assimilationists, I figured out how to make anybody like me. All I had to do was change to be like them.

I smiled or didn't smile. I learned to make jokes, or listen to my friends be sad. I found out what they liked—dogs or hiking, books or horses, and talked to them about that. I never cried, or told them anything about myself.

My brother was my only friend. When we were children, Jeffrey and I played in sprinklers in the hazy Los Angeles sun. We screamed as a golf ball unraveled its live coils, like a reptile hatching in the rose bed. We climbed a tower in the backyard and perched there all afternoon, told secrets, swore our undying allegiance to each other. When we were children, we had no friends save each other. We lay on the floors of our rooms talking life and death and dreaming of the galaxy. When we were children, we built a magic stone circle in the woods in the national park where we went camping each summer. For years we visited that circle, returning each summer to watch the slow erosion of stone by snow and wind. I was an intense, fire-haired child who wrote poems about volcanoes and water. He was a dark boy who wrote startling poems about his alienation from the world.

When my brother was about nine he came home from school and cried at the dinner table.

"Mommy, the kids teased me on the playground," Jeffrey said, huge tears clinging to the sides of his dark eyelashes. "They teased me about my nose."

"Your nose. Why would they tease you about your nose?" my mother asked.

"They said I look Jewish. Are we?" Jeffrey blurted, staring at my mother, a canned pea clinging to his fork.

"What? Of all the crazy . . . Of course not, Jeffrey. We are not Jewish. I've told you, we're agnostics. Besides, there is no such thing as looking Jewish. Arab people have noses like yours. Stop playing with your food. You too, Irene," she said, turning to glare at me. I'd been mushing the peas and meatloaf together in hopes of getting rid of the peas somehow. What scared me that day was that I could not read the look in her eyes.

It was the late 1960s. We were dreaming of infinity and the speed of light. When I thought of my future, I imagined myself in a space station, on a long journey across the milky way. Jeffrey and I played astronaut, simulated launches in our backyard. We watched *Star Trek* and *Space 1999*. If our parents had come west, it was another kind of escape we dreamed of: Space, the final frontier.

The year of the Apollo Moon Landing we were listening on the car radio as we headed for our summer camping trip. Everyone was silent as my father navigated the rough dirt road to Juniper Lake, concentrating, piloting a moon vehicle on a camping frontier. Then Neil Armstrong said, "One small step for a man; one giant leap for mankind," as we topped the last hill before the campground.

I imagined myself in giant boots striding through moon seas. I flung myself from the car and flew down the service road of the campground. The moon rose through the fir trees and hung over the volcano visible across the lake. I stopped—dust from my boots spiraling upwards behind me, moon dust, covering me in a fine film.

Clouds erupted out of the white mouth of the volcano. We set up our canvas tent next to the lake, under the immense sky. After dark, red lights traveled across that sky.

Then they stopped, suspended over the volcano. My father pointed, "There goes a satellite." I imagined a tiny satellite family with radios, watching us eat roasted spam in a can opened with a key.

I pictured nuclear warheads dangling on long strings from those gliding lights, saw them splash into the dark lake. The world ended. We lived on spam and never had to return to Los Angeles. My father's shaving cream melted as we, the last people on earth, hiked to the top of the volcano, watched an orange glow rise from the east, the south, everywhere.

The world did not end. I fell asleep in my sleeping bag with ducks on its red flannel lining, woke in the cold dawn to hear my mother snap the buttons on her Western shirt, pull on her black pants, as she snuck out for her morning hike. My mother wore those black pants every summer, until one day, when she told me they had stood up and walked away without her, into the fir and pine forest. I believed her. Part of me still believes my mother's pants are out there, walking through frost-rimmed meadows.

Deer were my mother's companions as she wandered while I pretended to sleep, knowing she was roaming through manzanita and lupine, strolling along the lakeshore in morning mist. One year my mother discovered bones by the lake's outlet. She thought they were deer bones. She had always wanted to find deer bones. My mother followed the deer, discovered their circular beds imprinted in the grass under fir trees, watched them eat breakfast in wet skunk cabbage marshes. She counted their fawns and worried about them when they crossed the boundary between the national park and the national forest, where they allowed hunting. But she had never seen them die, the deer, and she knew they must die. So she searched for their bones and finally found them.

She took the bones back to Los Angeles in a box, cleaned them with bleach, and brought them to a taxidermist, who told her they were not deer bones. They were cow bones. They were only cow bones—but she decided to keep them. She spray-painted them red. Those bones rested on our glass porch table as ornaments and my mother pretended she was Georgia O'Keeffe, painting bones in the desert.

My mother gave me no Jewish pride, nor sense of heritage. But she gave me a love for this earth, for the wide and dry endangered landscapes of California. A pagan she is, my small-framed, bookish mother, with strong legs that propel her up mountains in her seventies. "There's no place like California," she used to insist, as we drove in our station wagon on some Sunday excursion to the San Gabriel Mountains, to Joshua Tree, to Point Mugu, to one of those wonderful hidden places she'd researched.

"There's no place like California," she'd chant, swiveling to face me in the back seat, almost daring me to contradict her. "You have the mountains, the ocean, the desert, all within a few hours of each other. . . ." She'd be off on the speech I heard my whole childhood. I would stop listening, stare at her sullenly.

"But if only it would snow here," I'd whine.

My mother would tell me, her small daughter, how filthy the snow in the east became after a few days, how slushy it was on the streets. She'd praise the openness of Los Angeles, its low buildings, its wide freeways, so refreshing after the claustrophobia of vertical skylines. "And in California the roads are free!" she'd end happily. My father would smile at my mother then, as he piloted the blue station wagon north on the uncrowded smooth freeways of the 1960s.

My mother studied California, immersed herself in the literature of Austin, Krutch, and Muir, reading their stories to us in the car, where the open windows carried her words across the desert into the ears of hawks. She took us on pilgrimages to the parks: winter, spring, summer, fall. Each year we climbed the summit of Mount Piños. My mother would fling her taut body on the summit under ponderosa pines and proclaim, "Nature is my church." I'd lay next to her in the pungent needles, listening to the wind. Perhaps this was the closest I ever got to her.

Despite her proclamation that nature was her church, my mother, along with my father, decided to send my brother and me to Congregational Church school. At chapel every Friday the entire school sang "Onward Christian Soldiers." The kindergartners were too young to sing. They shouted out the words in the front pews of the church. "On-ward Christ-ian Sold-iers. March-ing as to War!" I memorized the books of the Bible. There were dark pews with maroon-colored velvet cushions, heavy hymn books, tiny pencils and nothing to draw on. There was an enormous organ. Sometimes I'd watch the organist's flushed face in his tiny mirror, or crane my neck to see his feet push pedals in the balcony high above us. There were stained-glass windows with scenes from the Bible. There were gruesome slide shows of the crucifixion, dark crosses under a foreboding sky. There was a vice-principal in a brown suit who spanked children who didn't do their homework. I lived in fear of him. There was fear in that school. Fear of the man in the brown suit. Fear of the crucifixion that terrified my brother and sent him home crying to my mother about how he was going to get burnt up in Hell.

I was a child who loved words. Perhaps the biggest word I remember knowing as a child was: agnostic. "We are agnostics, Irene," my mother told me, when I first came home from school asking what religion we were. "What's an agnostic, Mommy?" I asked. "It means we don't know if there is a God."

Agnostics? This uncertain belief system left room for doubt, but also for belief. But my mother also said, "When you're dead, you're dead. There's no such thing as heaven."

Like many assimilated Jews, my parents found some community in the Unitarian Church. I was baptized there, and remember the fear I felt as I was immersed in water, could not breathe. My memories are of itchy pink Sunday school dresses, Easter egg hunts, and sermons that bored or frustrated my parents, until one day they said we would not be going back.

There were a thousand palm trees in the city of my childhood. Their heads were gray, stained by smog. There was a brick house. There was a lighted kitchen in that house where I sat at a Formica table and would no longer look at my father. I was thirteen. My mother was growing her hair long and joining consciousness-raising groups. One night my father threw a glass at the wall behind my mother because she said she was going back to work. Then he lay on the floor of the living room in the dark, and wouldn't talk to anyone. I fled past him through the front door. Outside, the blooms of the oleander tree glowed pink in the dusk. I never went into that corner of the yard. When I swept the driveway I was careful not to let those poisonous leaves touch my hands. But sometimes, like that night, I wanted to cram handfuls of oleander into my mouth.

Why did I often eat dinner while imagining myself standing outside the window looking in at our family tableau? Did I sense the fractures in my parents' marriage spreading under the foundation of that brick house, the tension rising through the basement, seeping up into that yellow kitchen? I always watched my family from far away. I was a coyote in the hills, a skunk in the backyard, the possum my father drowned in a trap one winter. I was a stranger staring through a window, observing a family eat meatloaf in a cozy kitchen.

After eighth grade my brother and I went to separate Catholic schools. I attended Immaculate Heart High School, run by the Sisters of the Immaculate Heart of Mary, who were infamous for their feminist views on abortion, and a long history of activism in the civil rights and anti-war movements. I thrived in this liberal school, with its focus on encouraging the development of young women's self-expression, self-esteem, and independence. Although we were required to take twenty credits in religion, non-Catholic girls could choose from a variety of electives. For me, religion class meant a course on marriage in which I perused and analyzed *Ms. magazine* and developed my emerging feminism. It meant a class on "Population, Poverty and Hunger" that explored not only the existence of those epidemics, but also located their root causes in the unequal distribution of the world's resources, in the ills of capitalism and global corporatism. One Sister taught us about the occult. She drew astrological charts and showed slides of auras. I took an independent study in reincarnation, in which I read Alan Watts and other mystical thinkers, and debated my religion teacher on whether religion was necessary for a moral society. Although I was a shy girl, I also made it known that I was willing to debate anyone in the school on the existence of God, and spent lunch hours fervently discussing these questions with girls who were sometimes threatened by my agnostic beliefs.

I was sixteen. My mother's hair was long. She did not want to be called mommy anymore. "I am not mommy, I am a woman with a name," she told me. "Call me Claire."

My mother was worried I would get pregnant. I was not interested in boys but she was still worried. She took me to see her gynecologist. My mother was a feminist so she took me to see a woman. The nurse put me on the table and arranged my feet in stirrups. I was sweaty and afraid I smelled down there. I worried the gynecologist would tell me I was too fat. All doctors told me I was too fat. The gynecologist arrived and told my mother to leave the room. Now, here it comes, I thought. The doctor told me to sit up. She leaned close, put a kind hand on my shoulder.

"Irene, do you have a boyfriend?" she asked.

"Yuck."

"Well, are you interested in boys?"

"No way,"

She smiled. "Get dressed. Tell your mother that when you have a boyfriend I will fit you for a diaphragm. Not until then. I don't think she has anything to worry about."

Birth control. My brother and I volunteered at Planned Parenthood one Saturday. We walked around and around a big table, assembling birth control kits. One IUD, one package of pills, one condom, three little pamphlets, one diaphragm.

My mother read *Our Bodies, Ourselves*. She took me to a speculum demonstration organized by the Los Angeles Feminist Health Center. The speculum demonstration was in a movie theater. A woman sat on the edge of the stage and opened her legs. Women lined up to see her healthy pink cervix. I was mortified and refused to line up with my mother.

My mother and I got up at dawn to canvas for the ERA. I had never done anything political before. We left pamphlets on people's doors, presents for them to wake up to. This was a grand adventure.

I didn't shave my legs. Though my hair was pale blonde my friends at school noticed. I went out and bought a BIC razor, shaved my underarms and bought deodorant. I refused to shave my legs though. My mother called my hair my fuzz. She called me her fuzzy-wuzzy. But she told me my butt was too big.

I decided I would lose weight. I was 125 pounds and my mother was 110 pounds. I wanted to be thinner than my mother. I restricted myself to 800 calories a day. I counted apricots and apples, read yogurt labels. At first my mother was happy as I shed pounds. I admired my flat stomach in the mirror. I didn't tell my mother about feeling dizzy when I walked the two miles to school. I was happy when the scale read 108 pounds. My mother bought cherry pie for dessert. I refused to eat any. My mother agonized. "You're going to get anorexic, Irene," she cried. "Please," she begged, "Eat some cherry pie." "But you didn't want me to be fat!" I cried.

It would be too dangerous to write about how I held my pee as a child, how I held my pee for hours because my mother praised me for this ability, for never needing to go to the bathroom, how she called me her little camel, and I was proud of having no needs.

I held my pee and I held my tears. When did I decide to hold my tears, not to cry in front of my parents? Was it because I rarely saw either of them cry? Was it when my father banged his fist on the table, my brother burst into tears, and my father yelled, "Don't be so goddamned sensitive!"

It would be dangerous to write about the frosting, how I would creep down those cold, cement stairs to the freezer in the basement, where I would stand, armed with a knife, slicing chocolate frosting off frozen cakes. Only the frosting, never the cake itself. The freezer was my altar, this my act of worship, my act of self-hatred, my cry for help as I tried to cover my deed, to smooth down the frosting, knowing my mother would discover this mutilation, knowing I would deny it when she confronted me. This was a good girl's form of rebellion, this scarring of cakes.

I held my plump belly in. I pinched it in the tall mirror near the bathroom, sliced it off with the flat of my hand, sneered down at it when I sat on the toilet. I held my belly in, and with it my breath. I learned to breathe shallowly, without expanding that round belly outward. I learned to hold my belly in, hold my breath, my tears, my pee.

My mother's hair was way past her shoulders, wild and free. In the living room, the women talked of orgasms. Claire was reading Sheri Hite. She was reading Erica Jong. There was a picture on the cover of a woman with an unzipped, low-cut shirt. My mother said she was not afraid of flying. My father said he wanted his dinner by 6:00 p.m. He lay on the floor in the dark, crying. My parents went to therapy. The therapist leaned back and smoked his pipe while they fought. My brother and I went to therapy with my parents. My brother cried, but I didn't cry at all.

My father drove us home from therapy on the freeway in the dark. It was raining hard. We were somewhere in the San Fernando Valley. My brother and I were quiet. Suddenly the car filled with an awful sound. It was my father, sobbing. He pulled over to the shoulder of the road. Headlights pierced the inside of the station wagon. In the flashing lights, I could see my brother's open trembling mouth, my father's dark head in his hands. That terrible sound escaped from his throat, scraped at my belly. I wanted to unbuckle my seat belt, reach over and comfort this man who was my father, but he seemed miles away. It seemed we had always been sitting in the car beside the freeway, my brother and I, listening to our father cry.

Then I was angry. Why couldn't he keep driving through his tears? Why couldn't he control himself, the way I did, the way my mother did? She must have been home by then, wondering where we were, and here we were, stuck by the side of the road, with a father who was not acting like a father at all! Under his sobbing, I could hear the rhythm of the windshield wipers, back and forth, back and forth. Each approaching car caught us in its headlights, revealing our secret. What were the people in those cars thinking as they saw us by the side of the road? That we were a family in trouble, only those people probably just thought it was car trouble, not real trouble, big trouble like my brother and I were in, alone with our sobbing father.

I don't know how long we were there that night, by the side of the freeway. What I do remember is that my brother and I were silent as our father sobbed, and that neither of us touched him.

My father was standing in the doorway, blocking the entrance to the kitchen. Need radiated down from his slumped shoulders to his arms. He reached for me as I tried to brush past him to the breakfast table where my mother was waiting. I wanted the safety of my mother. But I couldn't go to my mother, sit down next to her where she was cracking her soft-boiled egg in its coiled metal egg cup, where she was sipping her cup of coffee, her small glass of orange juice. I couldn't go to my mother, because he, my father, was waiting for me, blocking my way. He wanted to hug me. He reached for me. He slung his arm over my freckled shoulders and jerked my body close to him. "I love you. I love you," he said, over and over, insisting: "I love you." When I did not answer him, his arm tightened over my shoulder, crept towards my neck. He shook me a little. "I love you so much, Irene, so much."

I stood stiff, straight as possible. I was counting to myself. One. Two. Three. Daddy, let go of me. I kept counting. I must, above all, avoid looking into my father's dark, wet eyes, I thought. If I look into his eyes I will fall into his love and never be able to climb out.

It all blurs together, the metallic smog of Los Angeles and the way I could never see the mountains, and the palm trees that shed their dead fronds in the pale sun, and how I felt fat and ugly and different from the other girls in high school, and my father's tears, and my silence, and my mother's yearning for freedom. My mother zooming ahead of us on Sunday afternoon hikes, while my father looked at his watch, granting her twenty minutes to fly.

My father left a note under the metal lamp on the desk in the study. "I'm going away for awhile so we can think about things." Now he tells me, "I never meant to leave permanently, to ask for a divorce. It was just a separation I wanted. But your mother wouldn't let me come back."

Was there grief in the jacaranda tree, in its heavy purple scent, in the bell-shaped flowers raining down in a purple bruised cloud onto the cracked pavement of the driveway? Was there grief in the round, hard pods that snapped, broke under our high tops? Did grief cling to the heavy golden drapes that shrouded the living room where my father lay on the floor and cried? Did grief spread its greasy film across the mahogany dining room table where we ate steak and fried tater tots each Sunday evening, and where my parents argued about oil drilling and Richard Nixon? Did grief hide under my bed, where I stretched out and dreamed dreams I can no longer remember? Did grief look at me in the mirror when I turned sideways and made faces at my big butt? Did grief lock my shoulders, twist my face away from my father's needy eyes?

After the divorce. A yellow frame house. The sound of avocados smashing onto the metal roof of the garage. Avocados buried in the ivy by the big red dog, who hoarded them when they fell, then wolfed them down late at night, while we slept.

The carpet was lime green. The street was lined with huge arcing leafy trees that I could never identify in the two years I lived there. I lay on the green carpet and dreamed of escaping somewhere out of the smog.

How do you describe smog, the way a girl can't breathe in it, how it shortens the lives of tires and clothing, corrodes elastic waistbands, how quietly it erodes your lungs too, makes them look as if you smoked your whole life? How do you describe smog, how it casts a gray cloak over your happiness, the stink of it, the industrial sting of it on eyeballs and throat, how it sucks the air out of a girl's chest when she runs, sends her to hide in a dark bedroom on a summer day?

How do you describe smog, the taste of it, metallic aftertaste on tongue and lips, the acidic kiss of it, the exhausted intimacy of it, the collective breath of it, the belly of it hanging low over the city, the weight of it? How do you describe smog, how it steals the sunset or ignites it with poisonous reds and yellows you know you shouldn't be breathing, and most of all, how it obscures the stars you hunger for, and only see on vacation. My brother pasted stars on his ceiling and I tacked a poster of the milky way galaxy above my bed. I would comfort myself with stories about the galaxy, and tell myself the universe was so big that no one would really care about a girl who weighed too much and read too many books.

My brother ran through those years. In his Budweiser T-shirt he ran through the heat and the smog, past the zoo and the horseback stables, through cemeteries, and under the eye of the observatory. He seemed to have no fear when he loped through those hot streets, his tanned, lean body contrasting with my roundness, his bravery contrasting with my shyness.

My brother also couldn't wait to learn to drive. At sixteen he bought a beat-up old Datsun, repaired it, and drove the freeways of Los Angeles out into the desert.

When I think of that yellow house where I spent the last years of my childhood, it is always summer, and I am always sprawled on the floor of my room eating chocolate mint space sticks and reading. My father is far away, on a greener, more humid coast. He writes me long letters in the perfect calligraphic handwriting he learned at French

Chapter I: The Past Was Not A Danger Here

Catholic boarding school in Turkey. "I want so much to be closer to you," he writes, and I read his letters and hate myself.

When I think of that house I am always alone, and it is always hot. A fan is humming somewhere. I hear the neighbor speaking in Japanese to his wife, who never seems to leave the house either.

The truth is, I do not remember much about that house at all, and the years I spent marooned there, in the aftermath of my parents' "civilized" divorce. My mother sold real estate and came home late some nights, tired and cynical from cold calls, carrying cold pizza for my brother and me.

I remember how my back ached after I lay on that floor reading for hours, listening for the sound of avocados falling from a great height, as if from another world.

II.

THE TRANSFORMATION OF SILENCE

"That visibility which makes us most vulnerable is also the source of our greatest strength."

—Audre Lorde

NICE JEWISH GIRLS

I graduated from high school only two months after my grandfather's funeral. In the cool redwood forests of the University of California, Santa Cruz campus, I, like my parents, turned my back on the pain of the past, the divorce, and remade my life. Preoccupied with crushes on women, as well as the pursuit of a college education in environmental studies, I gave little thought to my Jewish background until my last year in college.

I had a strong sense of myself as a lesbian, of lesbian oppression and existence. I read everything I could find about lesbian identity, so in 1982 I read *Nice Jewish Girls: A Lesbian Anthology.* I remember sitting in my dorm room engrossed for hours, as rain soaked the redwood forest outside my window. Evelyn Torton Beck wrote in her introduction, "Jewish invisibility is a symptom of anti-semitism as surely as lesbian invisibility is a symptom of homophobia." I questioned myself: If I was committed to being out as a lesbian, why wasn't I coming out as a Jew? But, with my complex, suppressed Jewish history, what did visibility mean? What Jewish territory was mine to claim? I came from no tradition of secular Jewish socialist activism in the Bund or the American labor movement. Steeped in familial cynicism about religion, I could not feel comfortable embracing Judaism and its rituals. It seemed to me then that the only Jewish landscape I could claim was the Holocaust itself. Thus I began to read and write intensely about those terrible years, searching for an understanding of my family's history and why they made the choices they did.

I read books about the Kindertransport that rescued 10,000 German Jewish children, including my mother and her sister, and brought them to safety in England. When I was a child I had read *The Diary of Anne Frank* and sobbed all night but I had no idea I was reading part of the history of my family, that I had a cousin who was hidden with her mother in Holland. I re-read the book, only this time it was my mother who was a child listening to jackboots, tracing with her eyes gashes of swastikas on familiar buildings, growing up in a country of fear.

It wasn't simply that I knew I was Jewish, and that everything was different. It was that I knew what it was to have been one thing, and then to be another. I knew what it meant to read books on the Holocaust as a non-Jew and then to re-read them as a Jew. In April, 1983 I wrote in my journal: "I saw Holocaust films as a Protestant and now I see them differently, knowing that I'm Jewish. Can we not know the other unless we *are* the other?" I wanted to understand the lives of women of color, and my own experience stepping from one world to another made me realize that I would never be able to truly cross that cultural barrier.

I graduated from college and shortly afterwards began to take workshops from feminist writers whose emphasis was on writing about personal experience. I began to explore my family's silences in my poetry and creative nonfiction.

In the mid-1980s, my growing identity as a child of Holocaust refugees oddly coincided with the increasing visibility and valorization of sadomasochism within the gay and lesbian community. In 1984, I stood at the Gay Pride march in San Francisco, watching the parade of men and women in chains and leather, carrying whips. So many of the blond and muscular men in their leather vests and pants celebrated militaristic fashion, an Aryan, Nazi aesthetic. It deeply upset me to read about and see lesbians who played Nazi/Jew in bed, who wore stormtrooper costumes and swastikas as part of sexual scenes.

Meanwhile, my intensive reading about the Holocaust was leading me to an understanding of how sadomasochism and pornography were central forces in Nazism. It became impossible for me not to speak out against the growing lesbian celebration of sadomasochism as a kind of liberation or freedom, and it seemed natural for me to articulate this opposition in writing. In 1985 I published an essay in booklet form, *Remember the Fire: Lesbian Sadomasochism in a Post-Nazi Holocaust Era* and distributed it through my feminist press, HerBooks. To my surprise, the essay received national attention, and was widely reviewed and quoted. My essay delved into an exploration of the ways that sadomasochism fueled the Holocaust, and the anti-semitic insult sadomasochism is to Jewish women.

"The sadomasochistic virulence of the Holocaust is deeply embedded in our most 'private' sexual selves." I wrote. "We live in a post Nazi-Holocaust world. We wear stormtrooper costumes, swastikas and play Nazi/Jew in bed. We call this making love. Even lesbians have not escaped. We too are caught in a great chain of history, a sadomasochistic chain which has persisted so long we have learned how to live with it, how to adapt to its weight, to walk differently, love differently, desire differently. We get used to it, so used to it we no longer notice it is there."

While "Remember the Fire" was primarily a passionate political essay articulating why an opposition to sadomasochism was a crucial feminist stance, it was also a narrative of my own family's forced assimilation, and my discovery of my own Jewish identity. I wrote for the first time of the silence that had shadowed my childhood: "I write these words against the weight of a silence generations deep. I have no resentment against my family for their silence; it is the silence of healing, of the snow of years falling softly, mercifully, on a withered family tree, on piles of disappeared relatives; the silence of fear, of survival. What do I do with these holes in history, these voids in the family tree? Will these words fill the silence?"

In that essay I grappled with my own identity as a Jewish woman, with a Jewish woman's body. I wrote of my Holocaust nightmares: "I'm dreaming. I dream I am standing by the side of a cattle car. Five old women lean out of the train and hand me their memoirs wrapped in dirty plastic, saying, 'Take these. Do something with them.' I know they are on their way to Auschwitz. I awake incredibly nauseous, and sit by the heater trying to get warm, arguing with these spirit women whom I have no doubt existed. I tell them I'm doing the best I can. I write. Finally, I go to sleep."

From that dream of five old women with diaries sprang my conviction that I am partly on this earth to tell my family's story, in this memoir.

ISRAEL

That same year, 1985, my Grananyu Margit took me to Israel on a ten-day TWA getaway tour. Ironically, my grandmother and I were among the few Jews on this bus tour composed mostly of born-again Christians coming to see the Holy Land. Though she never articulated it this way, perhaps this trip was her attempt to give me something of my Jewish heritage, some sense of pride in our people's history.

From the moment I set foot in Israel, a profound sadness seized me. I did not feel a sense of belonging, but rather felt isolated as a lesbian. I missed my lover. I was six thousand miles from home. I tried to hold back the tears, but finally broke down and cried in Jerusalem, in the bed I shared with my grandmother. I never cried in front of anyone then, and was alarmed that I had awakened her with my tears. What would happen now? She was impatient. "You have to be strong and not cry," she admonished me. "You are the same person everywhere. People all over the world are the same." I remember lying in that bed, the sun rising over that golden city of domes and light, as my grandmother whispered to me of her long journeys across the world. In her words, I began to get a glimpse of the strength it took to take that journey, the challenges of hanging on to some consistent sense of self despite her uprooted life. I marveled at her ability to see the commonality of humanity across cultures and nations.

I wish my grandmother had not told me to stop crying. I wish she had held me and stroked my forehead, let me cry my loneliness. Perhaps my tears were about more than missing my lover's touch and the kiss of fog on familiar redwoods; perhaps I somehow sensed the loneliness of my family's migrations and exiles, and perhaps I, unlike my grandmother, was able to cry.

Daughter of California's instant suburbs, I was captivated by the ancient history of Israel, so much more visible than the tribal history buried beneath Los Angeles. By the Sea of Galilee, framed by soft hills of golden grass sprinkled with black volcanic rocks, carpeted in vibrant purple thistles and oak trees, my grandmother and I walked arm-in-arm. I was twenty-four then. My grandmother and I had not yet developed the closeness we would develop before her death. Still, I felt so drawn to this woman whose life spanned the century, this woman who whispered to me, "I think we have the same spirit. In so much we are the same."

My grandmother and I traveled through Israel. We also traveled to the past, to the Holocaust. It was on that trip that I heard much of her life story for the first time: of her brother Imre who refused to convert and was deported, of her uncles whom she tried to warn about the Nazis but who would not listen and were murdered, of her cousin shot outside the synagogue in the town square. "Before the war I came from a big family. I had forty eight cousins," she told me, "but afterwards only ten were left, and the family was scattered across the world, from Australia, to Chile, to London." By day we traveled through Israel, at night we sat in our hotel room and reckoned with the past.

Together we went to Yad Vashem, walking under trees planted in honor of Righteous Gentiles who helped Jews during the Holocaust, into the museum itself. We did not walk through the museum together. I left my grandmother, and forged ahead stoically through an exhausting exhibit of bureaucratic documents from the first phase of the Nazi project, which eliminated the civil rights of Jews in order to drive them out of Germany. This was the most chilling exhibit for me: documents prohibiting Jews from walking certain streets, from using public parks, attending public schools. Yellow stars from six different countries. ID cards branded "J."

I was mostly numb in that museum. There were too many statistics. I stood before a display about the shooting of Jews by firing squads in the fields. In a caption, a Nazi guard described a grandmother soothing a crying child just before the people were to be shot, and he described the people standing quietly, as if this was a normal event, waiting to be shot. I looked at the picture in that display and I saw how much the women in that picture looked like my Jewish friends at home. I remember thinking: *these people were real.* This really happened. I almost cried then, but I looked behind me and saw my small 85-year-old grandmother tenaciously making her way through the exhibit. I pushed my tears away.

Now I wish my grandmother and I had walked through that exhibit together, that I could have held her arm then, and witnessed her grief. Perhaps it would have been too painful for her to share this with me, whom she wanted to protect from this history. Perhaps I sensed that. Really, I had no idea how she coped with her grief, and so I avoided the whole subject. We went alone through that museum, without each other's comfort. We never spoke of it.

I was not romantic about Israel. I was well aware of its political complexities, its militaristic culture, the homophobia I sensed there. Much of the trip was painful and lonely for me. And yet, as the years have passed, I have grown more and more grateful to my grandmother for our journey. In Israel, I was given a visceral sense of Jewish history. Despite the complexities, I did feel a sense of awe and pride in the ancient and enduring culture of a people I increasingly saw as *my people*.

Several years after my grandmother and I took that trip to Israel, I became lovers with a Jewish woman for the first time. I took Tina to meet my grandmother. When we walked into my grandmother's house, Tina turned to me and whispered, "It smells like grandmother in here." Was it some mixture of cold cream and cabbage, old-world kitchen? At first my grandmother was awkward, turning to ask me, "What does *she* do?" But then she looked at Tina and said, "You are my kind, my dear. I can be myself with you." "Good," my lover said. Then my grandmother said, "You have a Jewish face like mine, not like Irene, who does not look Jewish."

I remember my pain when she said that. With these words my grandmother was both praising me and rejecting me. She always took pride and comfort in my red hair and pale skin, probably because she felt they would protect me from anti-semitism. And yet she was bonding with my lover over their Jewishness. I felt abandoned.

In the late 1980s, I also published through HerBooks, *Bubbe Meisehs by Shayneh Maidelehs an Anthology of Poetry about Jewish Grandmothers by Their Granddaughters,* edited by the Jewish lesbian writer, Lesléa Newman. Publishing this anthology gave me a new appreciation for my grandmother's life as a Jewish woman, the complexities and contradictions of her Jewish identity, and the importance of recording and documenting her story in my writing. I began to realize that despite my grandmother's desire to assimilate, and her acquiescence to my parents' wishes to hide their Jewish background from their children, she still had a great deal of cultural pride. Indeed, it was her decision to give her husband a Jewish burial, which "spilled the beans" about our family's history.

GRIEF FOR LOST WORLDS

Not knowing I was Jewish until I was seventeen was, and to some extent still is, the most salient feature of my Jewish identity. At seders, I always felt the need to explain my peculiar history: "I'm Jewish, but I didn't find out until I was seventeen," I would explain, somehow feeling that I needed to say this before partaking of matzoh, sitting down to read the *Haggadah*. I didn't want to be mistaken for a non-Jew, was aware that my red hair and fair skin could easily confuse things. But I was also afraid that my ignorance of

Jewish tradition was so obvious that were I assumed simply to be Jewish, I would quickly betray myself in some horrible *faux paus*.

Perhaps what I felt was shame. Friends tried to reassure me that they, too, were uneducated about Judaism. They had grown up in assimilated families where Jewish holidays were rarely celebrated, and then only in the shallowest way. But I wore my shame. I felt like an impostor, caught between Jew and non-Jew—never at home in either world.

But what I felt and still feel is deeper than shame, which is, after all, a personal thing. What I carry inside is sharp, painful and engulfing grief—a collective wailing, a cross-generational mourning, wordless, dream-like. Perhaps I mourn for lost worlds, a devastated continent, the world of my great-grandmothers? Beneath the *Shoah* run the even older waters of Spain and Portugal, the blood of the Inquisition. Far below that the Temple is falling, and always, my people are in exile. I speak to you of grief and shame, but really there are no words for this loss. There is a howling, an endless wind, the grinding of continents, the light that is lost long before it can reach the deepest part of the ocean, but life somehow survives there, pale and blind, writhing with a desire to live.

I ate the sweet *charoses*, the bitter sharp horseradish, drank my cups of grape juice, partook of the richest kugels. I tried to be matter of fact, ordinary about my Jewishness. But I always felt set apart by this grief.

For a time I thought perhaps it would be easier if I simply explored being a cultural Jew, left aside questions of

God, religious observance. I joined *Kolaynu*, the Santa Cruz chapter of New Jewish Agenda, and pondered the complexities of Arab and Jewish relationships. I attended a study group on Melanie Kaye-Kantrowitz and Irena Klepfisz's anthology *The Tribe of Dina*. There were fervent discussions on Israeli politics, war in Lebanon, Palestinian exile, Jewish women in the trade union movement, Emma Goldman, Rosa Luxembourg. But there, too, I felt my ignorance and shame and always my grief, following me, my own personal watchdog, baring its teeth between me and any relaxed, expressive Jewishness.

What I felt most comfortable with in those years was immersing myself in learning about the Holocaust. I read historical accounts, novels, poetry, and memoirs of camp survivors. I watched every film about the Holocaust that came to town. I learned the history of the rise of Nazism in detail, year by year. I read the poetry of Irena Klepfisz, over and over, tracing her life as a child survivor, startled by Irena's physical resemblance to my mother.

CHILDREN OF HOLOCAUST SURVIVORS

I began to call my parents Holocaust refugees, to see myself as a daughter of two Holocaust refugees, to name what had been nameless my entire life. I knew what my parents had experienced was far less traumatic than those whose parents had been in the concentration camps. Still, my parents' and grandparents' lives had been profoundly affected by being born Jewish in Nazi Europe, and by their escape from the land of their birth. I began to understand the origins of the anxiety, fear, and overprotectiveness I had been raised with, as well as my family's tremendous passion for life.

In 1987, my friend Jeanne told me about a group called the Jewish Lesbian Daughters of Holocaust Survivors (JLDHS) which several friends of hers on the East Coast had founded. I remember thinking, if there ever was a group for me this must be it. On a visit to Jeanne in Boston, I participated in an afternoon poetry reading of JLDHS. Afterwards we all went out for dinner. I remember sitting at a long table filled with women, lesbians whose families had been in Nazi Europe, who shared my history. Some had parents who were concentration camp survivors; some had parents who had survived in hiding; others, like mine, had been refugees. When I told my story, the others listened with compassion and interest. All of them had been raised with knowledge of their Jewishness, so I was still different, even here. But these daughters understood the depth of the trauma my parents had experienced, and why it led them to conceal their past from their children. Here, I also felt a kinship with women who were first-generation Americans— the first native speakers of English in their families, who were raised without fast food and sometimes brought odd lunches to school (Mine were enormous turkey legs. I envied the other girls with tuna fish or peanut butter and jelly sandwiches). Here, too, were women who understood my nightmares, my reading obsessions, my terror of crying about the Holocaust. I was afraid, I told the women that afternoon, that if I started crying I would never stop. They understood.

It would be ten years until I was able to attend a JLDHS retreat, but just knowing this group existed gave me solace, a sense of belonging.

This memoir is my contribution to the storytelling by the Second Generation, a storytelling which child of Holocaust survivors Joseph Skibell calls, "a healing art, a medicinal practice . . . sacred healing." Hasidic teaching says the three stages of mourning are tears, silence, and song. "The Second Generation is in its final stages of mourning, says psychologist [Eva] Fogelman. They've gone through shock, denial, and confrontation. Now comes a search for meaning. Children of survivors who go through these phases eventually have a need to do something with these feelings," she says. "Second Generation writing is part of that search for meaning. It is their song."

INDIAN AND JEW, LOVING ACROSS WORLDS

For years, what I knew of spirituality I learned from my partner Valerie Jean, and what she shared of her Desert Cahuilla tribal culture with me. It was she who taught me that the dead come to visit. Perhaps they shake your feet when they are not pleased with you; perhaps they arrive in the shape of birds. Perhaps they come in dreams. Thus, long before I knew the Torah is sung by my people, I knew about oral tradition, stories preserved in song.

Valerie Jean's grandmother, Tutu, always came out of her house laughing. "*Míyaxwe*," she would greet us with her hello, hugging us close, then stepping a few feet back to look us over. We never told her we were lovers, but she seemed to be comfortable as long as we didn't use the word: lesbian. "You two girls take good care of each other," she used to say. They had the same laugh, Valerie Jean and Tutu, the same full smiles and wide hips, only Valerie Jean was a little taller. Tutu walked slowly, like Margit. In the last year of her life she kept an oxygen tank in a corner of the living room, and diabetic and heart medications on the table. On the living room wall was a set of shelves with a whole population of dolls. There was a built-in cabinet packed with black pottery.

Once she caught me looking at those shelves. I blushed.

"You like my dolls and pots? Took me years to collect those. Those dolls are katchina dolls, from the Hopis. The pots are from Santa Clara Pueblo. My friend made 'em. I used to go to all the pow wows before I got sick. My husband and I used to go together. Did you notice the baskets?" she asked.

I hadn't.

Tutu pointed at the coffee table. "My mother made those."

I looked at the three baskets filled with rust-red feathers.

"Red-tailed hawk feathers," Tutu said. "Want to hold the baskets?" She got up. Valerie Jean started to protest that Tutu wasn't supposed to be jumping up and down like this, but Tutu got up, brought one of the baskets over for us to touch. "This one's my favorite. See the rattlesnake?"

My fingers traced the path of the sleek diamond-backed snake woven around the golden basket.

"That was my mother's favorite, too. This design is called *Séwet* in Cahuilla," Tutu explained, carrying the basket back to the coffee table, moving aside a stack of issues of *News from Native California*. "The brown part is deer grass, which is hard to gather now. The black part is juncus rush, dyed in an iron pot filled with elderberry leaves, nails and anything else iron you can find. Used to take over a week to dye the juncus that way. My mother made many more baskets but they all got lost. She was famous for her baskets."

"What happened to the other baskets, Tutu?" Valerie Jean asked gently.

"Well, some of them burned up in that fire my sister went through twenty years back. Most of them were sold for money over the years. White people like Cahuilla baskets. My mother's baskets are in museums all over the country, and even in Europe, I hear. I saw one myself once, up in Palm Springs at that museum they have there, under glass, of course. They always put the baskets under glass, and they cry."

"The baskets cry?" Valerie Jean asked.

"Yes, they cry because they aren't being used. They miss their people. That basket up in Palm Springs talked to me. It was a beautiful red and black one with an eagle design, a *big* one." She held her square hands out wide. Her hands looked like Valerie Jean's, long strong fingers, short nails, thick bones. "I thought about talking to the museum people about that one, to see if I could take it home, or to our museum at Malki, but I know they'd never believe that it was my mother's. Just some crazy old Indian lady. Half the time they think I'm Mexican, anyway." She laughed, "Of course it didn't have my mother's name on it."

As Tutu talked, I remembered camping in Anza Borrego State Park near Torres-Martinez reservation. I remembered my father Ernie's face, foamy with cream as he shaved at the edge of the picnic bench, under the portable awning. I remembered complex constellations suspended over the campfire at night, how I lay in the canvas tent and pictured nameless Indians gathering water in the canyon, in the far away past. All the while, Tutu and her people were living a few miles away. I had no idea they were even there. In fourth grade I had studied Indians, like every California child, constructed a tiny diorama of a Mission in a white shoebox—a puddle of glue for water, plastic cows, a green plastic fence, white buildings fashioned out of my father's shirt cardboards. I had been proud of that diorama.

One Memorial Day weekend, Valerie Jean and I went to Malki Days, a fiesta on the Morongo Reservation. It was cooler up there at the Pass than in the surrounding desert. The previous night, snow frosted the tops of Mount San Gorgonio and Mount San Jacinto, which gleamed in the sun thousands of feet above us. We met some of Valerie Jean's relatives. We rested with them in yellow lawn chairs in the shade and enjoyed the fiesta, which took place in a large open dirt area surrounded by ramadas.

The Cahuilla Bird Singers are what I remember most about that day, although there were many songs and many dances, and lots of good barbecued beef, homemade tortillas and beans. The Bird Singers told the story of how the Cahuilla people journeyed around the world six times before they settled down, and chose southern California as their home.

"That was when animals and people could still talk, you see," one of the Bird Singers said. The desert wind whirled through the gap between the mountains, blew loudly into the mike, almost drowning out his words, "The Bird Songs tell the story of our migration. We've been in this area for over six thousand years, here in southern California."

Someone leaned over and giggled, "He's been singing those songs for so many years. I remember when he was just a little boy."

I listened to the songs, to the gourd rattles filled with palm seeds, watched the young girls learning to hop from foot to foot in tiny steps, to dance like birds. I couldn't understand the words, but part of me understood the migration story, the story of another desert people.

Valerie Jean told me seders reminded her of ceremonies on the reservation where everyone got together and told the Creation story. "But Cahuillas don't make you wait to eat." she would laugh. "I think Jews are a tribe too, Irene," she said once. "Another tribe from the desert."

Maybe she was right, I remember thinking. Jews are a tribe scattered all over the world with a long history, with stories passed down since when we lived in the desert four thousand years ago. And now are Indians beginning their Diaspora, so many of them exiled from their original land?

We loved for eight years across our worlds, of Indian and Jew, she immersing herself in klezmer music, seders, and the words of Holocaust survivors; I reading Native American literature, helping to organize the first Indigenous California Women's Conference at UC Santa Cruz in 1992. Both of us were raised by assimilated mothers; both of us struggled with recovering our heritage.

Sometimes it was not so easy, loving across those boundaries of race. There were moments when my class and race privilege stood in stark contrast to her working class childhood and family. There were painful times when we disintegrated into comparing oppressions. But for the most part, this aspect of our eight-year partnership was marked by a tremendous exchange as we supported each other on our separate journeys. I did not become a want-to-be Indian, but rather deepened my thirst to know about my own people's ceremonies, songs, and history. There was a remarkable way in which, standing completely outside my agnostic, cynical upbringing, I could suspend my disbelief in spirits, in the spirit world. That experience provided the foundation for me to begin to explore Jewish spirituality, though it would take a few years before I started doing that in earnest.

A TRANSPORTED LIFE: THEA FELIKS EDEN

This story would not be complete if I left out my friendship with Thea Feliks Eden. When Valerie Jean first introduced me to her friend Thea in 1988, I remember feeling magnetically drawn to this small, composed woman with gorgeous reddish brown hair piled up elegantly on her head. The moment I heard her speak, her voice with its odd mix of British and German inflections electrified me, washed over me like family, so similar to the voices of my mother and aunt.

I had known Thea was a Holocaust refugee, but I had not been prepared for the intense feelings her presence inspired in me. Thea was about my mother's height and size. She had the same wild, long curls which were unusual in women in their early sixties. I stood next to Thea in a kitchen in Mill Valley. I shook her hand politely. I desperately wanted to tell her how much she reminded me of my own mother, but respected her obvious reserve. Besides feeling electrified, my strongest memory of that evening is sitting around after dinner in the living room playing with a package of plastic P4 polymer globules designed to help house plants stay moist. The globules swell up and retain water. They were new on the market and quite a novelty. We spent half the evening dumping slippery blobs into larger and larger water glasses, seeing how much bigger they would swell, laughing like maniacs. Thea had a wicked, throaty laugh that burst through her British reserve—the laugh of an escape artist.

What I didn't know that first night was that our meeting would be the only time I would see Thea completely well. Shortly after her return home she began to experience the strange dizziness and weakness that eventually developed into the paralysis which afflicted her until her death from breast cancer. I did get to know Thea much better over the next six years. Valerie and I went to visit her many times. In the early years when Thea could still walk, we went to the botanical garden. I stood close to Thea under a small redwood tree in the garden. She reached out to stroke the tree's soft, dark bark, expressed her admiration for the way redwood trees survive logging and fire to sprout new growth in rings around the stumps of their ancestors. The symbolism in her admiration for those survivor trees was not lost on me.

Strangely enough, I don't remember the first time I told Thea my parents were Holocaust refugees. What I do know is that as the years passed, we had many intense conversations about her life history and the parallels with my mother's. Thea was less than a year older than my mother. Both of them were born in Germany and were part of the Kindertransport program. Like my mother, Thea was a feminist all of her life, an outspoken, strong woman ahead of her time. Like my mother, Thea chose to have a child when she was 33, unusual at that time. But unlike my mother, who was reunited with her parents in the United States in 1940, Thea's mother was murdered by the Nazis. Thea said goodbye to her on her 13th birthday and never saw her again, a loss which haunted her for the rest of her life.

Thea never rejected her Jewish identity, although she chose carefully with whom she would share her life story, and she never considered herself a religious Jew. Only in the last year of her life did she occasionally light the candles and say prayers for Shabbat. The conversations I shared with Thea deepened my understanding of the people and history I come from—the world of Holocaust survivors, of refugees, of displaced people. Like my mother, Thea had a deep passion for the landscapes of California: the sea, the folded chaparral-covered mountains above Santa Barbara, such an ever-present backdrop above the red-tiled roofs of the town. One of her greatest desires was to see Yosemite, and Valerie, Thea, and I often dreamed of how we would travel there together.

Even when she was paralyzed and very ill, we would sit and try to figure out whether she could make a trip there in the van she had specially designed for herself to take trips in a wheelchair. But we never made it there together, to stand under Yosemite Falls and feel the spray on our faces, to watch the sunset illuminate Half Dome over the Merced River. Each time I go to Yosemite, I think of her.

In October of 1989, Thea and I collaborated on an oral history of her life, *A Transported Life*, which I published through HerBooks in 1995, after her death. She felt it was important to document the history of the Holocaust, particularly what happened to the children, a story that has not often been told. It was through talking with Thea that I began to get a glimmer of the deeply traumatic effects the Holocaust had on children, and how this post-traumatic stress manifested itself in my parents' choice to disassociate from their Jewish backgrounds altogether.

My relationship with Thea was a two-way mirror. For me, wrestling with issues of loss of heritage and the suppression of memory, Thea was a riveting and inspiring guide through some of the historical events that had affected my mother: Kristallnacht, everyday life in Nazi Germany, Kindertransport. She told me the stories my own mother could not tell me. For Thea, I was a witness. More than that, I was another daughter. The relationship between Thea and her daughter was complex, and it was not always easy for them to discuss Thea's past.

I often dream of Thea, even now after her death. Our connection seems to me paradoxical—filled with the words of rational, intellectual conversation, but also subterranean, dream-like. When we sat together, I often felt pulled by the undertow of an unspoken, shared grief. I was deeply inspired by her strength, humor, and passion for life. And through Thea, I came to know that it was time for me to talk to the members of my own family.

III.

DANCING THE CHARDAS:
MY GRANDMOTHER'S STORY

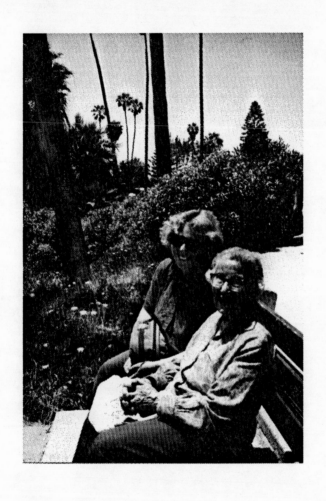

THE HAPPY AND SAD IN THE SAME SONG

"Come, we will sit down," my grandmother said. "You set the table so fine! Everything what is important, you remembered. Do I want anything else? Sure. I want my *azu*, my wine I want, not too much, only pour me a little. Yes that's right. Now we will drink and look into each other's eyes and wish each other the utmost happiness and best wishes. Oh, that is very fine, this wine! You know I need nothing but to look on you my granddaughter, to be happy. You are the continuation of my life, you and your brother."

She looked at her watch. "What time have you? Seven o'clock? One hour we have until *Lawrence Welk*. With *Lawrence Welk*, we can have ice cream with whipped cream. Just a little whipped cream. You know life has to have some sweetness. I am a sweet girl. So I am 93 years old? I am still a sweet girl.

"I read beautiful poems in my communication class. It is for the old people here that I go in this class. They understand me well. They see my struggle with English and try to help me. I believe I can succeed. The poems of Emily Dickinson, the novels of Crane, Garland, I read with interest. Have you read these books? Yes? Good.

"My philosophy class ended. It was very interesting and now I devote myself to the painting. I paint what I feel of trees, young men moving joyously, old ladies' faces. Look at that painting. No, not that one, the one above the couch. The face of my old lady has a little ironic smile, the eyes are courageous-looking, no?

"You read Elie Wiesel." She leaned forward. "I was in 1938 in Hungary with my son. My family which was all intellectuals, physicians, attorneys, very patriotic men couldn't believe that they will be touched. Very few survived. My great physician uncle and his wife took their life with terrible heroism before the Nazis could deport them. We few survivors now live in different and distant parts of the world from Australia to London, Canada, and Israel. Our scattered family.

"What else do I do? I read and swim. I go for the mild exercise class and rhythmically move with music. I like to sing with this music. I hear lectures about Camus and Machiavelli. History gives me much to think about. The world's happenings are very mysterious, chaotic. We can only choose an activity in which we give to the world, or better our community. Do you understand? Yes? Good.

"Now. Tell me, what is new in your life? Everything I want to know. Working at the library. That is a big job, a very big job. And what do you do for pleasure? Do you go dancing? Good, that is very good. When I was a young girl I liked so much dancing the *chardas*, so fast I would dance. You know I was too serious when I was a young girl, too much thinking. It is good that you dance.

"I am grateful to God, that my granddaughter feels life is good. I feel a deep responsibility for my followers: my son, granddaughter, grandson, great-grandson. I want them happy and when that is denied for me I am frustrated.

"You know, I was just thinking, sitting here looking at you, that this is a different world you live in. Sometimes I say to myself, Margit, you are 93 and living in Laguna Hills, California. How can this be?

"You like that painting? I painted that one on my trip to Canada after my husband died. I traveled there alone and stayed in a beautiful cottage by the lake. Sure I went alone. I was only 78 then. Alone by that lake I was and the wild wind was blowing that dark red tree and the water. That blue is the color of my soul.

"What time is it? Only 7:30. We still have half an hour. Put some music on. You do it so well. Your father, when he comes, also plays music. From when he arrives, to when he leaves, we have a concert. Sure you can play the Hungarian tape. Oh, that one has your grandfather's favorite song, the one about the roses trembling, falling from the bush, dying on the ground. You know he was a little melancholic, your grandfather. I was always trying to stimulate him, to cheer him up. He loved me for this. And here comes the *chardas*. Listen to how the mood changes. Hungarians are too sensible to be sad for too long. Yes, you are right, both the happy and the sad are in the same song."

THE HUNGARIAN CLUB

In her nineties, my grandmother was the vice-president of the Hungarian Club of Orange County. Once, when I came to visit, she and her best friend Anya took me to a Hungarian Club picnic.

In the car Anya said, "I would not have gone to this picnic if you were not going, Margit. I wanted to meet your granddaughter, this granddaughter I've heard so much about. I was born in Hungary. But I am *not* Hungarian. I hate Hungarians."

My grandmother sat up straight in the seat beside her. "I tell you, my dear. You are a Hungarian Jew."

"When the Nazis came I was not Hungarian. I was a Jew," Anya insisted.

I could tell this was an old argument between them. I kept quiet, looked out the car window at wide streets lined with lawns, white stucco houses, the Ralph's where Grananyu bought her groceries, lugged them home on the bus in two mesh bags. Ralph's, where she got in line one day to pay, didn't see that another woman was ahead of her, and the woman called her "Stupid Jew." My grandmother told me that story so many times. We drove past the Temple. It looked just like the eye doctor's office next door, except for the Jewish star pasted on the front.

"Are you Jewish?" Anya's watery blue eyes stared at me from the rear view mirror. I felt my face get hot. If I said yes, would Anya ask me to go with her to Temple? Wait a minute, she must know I'm Jewish. I am Margit's granddaughter. Maybe she wanted to hear me say it. Maybe she wanted to know where my loyalties were. She had survived two years in Auschwitz; I could understand why she wanted to hear me say it. So I smiled at her, "Of course." Her shoulders relaxed. She turned her eyes back on the road.

Rock Creek Park. The Hungarians waited in a far corner under tall maple trees. Anya, Margit and I stepped out of the car and made our way slowly across the grass. Immediately, a large woman with curly, brown, short hair strode up to us. She greeted Anya and Margit with a torrent of Hungarian, and then turned to me, speaking warmly. I couldn't understand a word she was saying.

"I'm very sorry but I only speak English."

"It's fine. Welcome. I am so glad to meet Margit's granddaughter."

This was the routine throughout the afternoon, me confessing, "I don't speak any Hungarian, I'm sorry," them reassuring me and praising my grandmother, the oldest woman here, and clearly one of the most beloved.

I smiled at everyone. Hungarian flowed all around me. I floated in the eddies, caught a word here and there as it rushed by: *very good, no, yes,* not much else. Sometimes I felt if I'd just changed channels, I could have understood everything they were saying.

We sat down at a picnic table under a maple tree. I brought Anya and Margit plates of hot, spicy goulash dished up by a tiny woman with clanking white plastic bracelets and a shrill voice. We drank 7-Up. Dessert was Winchell's donuts, chocolate-glazed. No Hungarian apple pie, no poppy seed pastry. I was disappointed.

After we ate, Magda, a woman with waist-length black hair and rosy cheeks announced, "Now it's time to play games!" I searched for a tree to disappear behind, but realized I was the youngest one there. I had to play. Magda asked all the women to line up on the grass. The men sat watching.

"Now kick your shoe off," she said enthusiastically.

"What do you mean, kick your shoe off?" they asked.

"Kick your shoe. Here, I'll demonstrate." Magda slipped her shiny yellow sandal halfway off, and kicked it into the parking lot from the lawn, a good twenty feet. "Okay? Let's kick our shoes. One. Two. Three."

I looked down at my feet, at all the women's feet lined up together. I realized I was the only one wearing black leather tennis shoes. I had tried so hard to look respectable for Grananyu, bought burgundy dress pants, a white shirt, and a gold and black vest just for this occasion. But I forgot about the shoes. I lifted my leg, kicked. My shoe landed about a foot away, upside down in the dirt. In the parking lot was a collection of ladies' yellow, red, and white sandals with small heels.

I glanced at Grananyu, sitting on the lawn chair I had set up for her, close by so she could watch. She was laughing. She was having a really good laugh, white head thrown back, glasses flashing in the sun, cheeks picking up the color of her red Hawaiian dress. Then I knew I was doing this for her. So, I threw water balloons, and carried a raw egg between my teeth on a plastic white spoon across the park, the only one who dropped the egg on the grass. I was one of two people who dropped their water balloons right away. It was just like high school volleyball, when I ducked as the ball came towards me. I did it all for my grandmother, to see her laugh.

Anya drove us home, and came in for tea and cookies. She talked about her son, a famous violinist in Cleveland. Margit said maybe she would study music next. Anya got mad, said Margit was 93, too old to learn anything new. Margit sat up straight on the couch and said sternly, "My dear, it is never too late."

Anya sighed, "My dear, you are always an optimist." Then she got up to leave, and I kissed her, once on each cheek lightly, European-style.

My grandmother and I decided to nap for a couple of hours. But I couldn't sleep. Planes from the nearby Air Force Base blasted over her house. When my grandmother had moved to her condo twenty years earlier she had been required to sign a release form saying she wouldn't complain about the planes. She claimed she didn't hear them anymore.

I tiptoed out to the living room at 5:30, when I'd promised to wake Grananyu. She was lying on the couch under a blanket, head tipped back, glasses off, snoring loudly. I watched her for a long moment. She was so pale. Her hair was so white. There were loose flaps of skin on her brown arms, and big moles. So many wrinkles on her face. She looked old. She looked like she was 93. When she was asleep, not telling stories or laughing, I could see just how old she was. I was scared, standing there in my grandmother's living room next to her cabinet with green china peacocks, her mother's ostrich feather fan. What if I was hovering there and Grananyu stopped breathing, had a heart attack? What if she just decided to die, right then, before dinner?

I crossed the room, sat down, touched her shoulder gently, not wanting to startle her awake. Her eyes flew open quickly, instantly alert. Then she saw it was only me, her granddaughter. She smiled. "Oh, I was so good sleeping." She lifted herself up on the couch slowly, stretched, reached for her glasses. We sat for awhile and then got up and warmed dinner in the oven.

A platter of meatloaf, potatoes, mushrooms, and carrots—all of it bland. I was not very hungry after the goulash I had eaten. But my grandmother insisted, "Take some more from the carrots. You did not have any mushroom. Take from the mushroom. It's very good. And the meat. You have to take from the meat. I prepared it with this special sauce." Then she realized she was doing what my father always told her not to do—telling people how much and what to eat.

"No. You have to eat how much you want," she said firmly. "I will not tell you what to eat. Here in America is freedom. Everybody eats what they want."

I studied her face quickly. Was she serious, or was that irony I heard in her voice? She couldn't really believe this stuff about freedom. But there she sat, just eating her potatoes.

MARGIT'S STORY

In 1994 I spent several days with my grandmother at my father's house, taping her life story. Before we began to talk, we needed to eat lunch. I went to the refrigerator. My grandmother carefully made her way over to the kitchen, stood next to the trash compactor. She held onto the counter with her small brown hands, thick with ropy veins.

I peered into the refrigerator, looked past a bowl of cranberry sauce, chicken legs in wrinkled foil. Way in the back I found plain yogurt. I opened the small container, pulled two bowls out of the cabinet. I told my grandmother to sit down, but she said she didn't want to, she wanted to help. I handed her two bananas to carry to the table.

My grandmother watched me spoon the white yogurt into the bowls. "Put some jam in it," she said, "Life has to have something a little sweet."

I found two cups in the cupboard above the electric can opener neither of us could work, and boiled water for tea. "Put an ice cube in the tea so it will not be so hot," my grandmother suggested.

I brought two red, quilted place mats and placed them on the round table. "You make it very nice," she said.

I looked out the window into the smoggy valley below my father's condominium. At the window a hummingbird hovered, listening. Far away the freeway cut through the hills, as some river might have, long ago, but since I was with my grandmother I did not care about the freeway, and how I was in the shrouded gray city of my childhood. I did not feel lost.

My grandmother said, "How beautiful! How beautiful."

I looked to see what she had found to admire here in this city of ugliness, and saw her gazing into the smog-filled valley at the pink flowers of the oleander hanging on the hillside. I saw what beauty was left here, at the end of my grandmother's life, and I bent to eat the yogurt with strawberry jam.

Then we began to talk about her life.

"I began medical school in Budapest, where I went for one year. Then came a time of more anti-semitism. This was even before Hitler. They said no more Jews could go to the school. I said to myself, I have many friends here who are not Jewish. They will help me. Nothing will happen to me. All the other Jews had left as refugees, but I stayed. I was the only one. I sat down between my friends. At once I heard a very disgusting sound from the student in back of me. Then the person who made this rude noise said, 'Don't you feel it? The air is not clean here. Somebody is here who makes our air not clean.'

"Humiliated, I decided to go to Vienna and try to attend medical school. My father refused to give me, a woman, money to go to medical school. I defied him, with the help of my Uncle Erwin, who was also a doctor. I took the train to Vienna. But in Vienna there were so many Jewish refugees already that all the quotas were filled. There was no place for me. I wrote to my parents, 'I have to go to Prague. In Prague they will take me.' My father wrote back, 'Go wherever you want. I will not send you a penny.'

"My father, Jakab, wanted me to just get married. 'A woman doctor,' he jeered, 'You must be crazy.' My mother, Regina, wanted me to be a doctor. She wrote me secretly that her whole ambition was for her daughter to be a doctor. But she had no money of her own to send me. My Uncle Erwin sent money again, and I went to Prague.

"In Prague I fell in love with chemistry. There were not enough places for all the Jewish refugees in the chemistry lab. But the lab teacher liked me. I was a smart young girl who wanted to learn. He said, 'There is a young man who did not keep his place. You can have his stool.' I studied chemistry all year. Then came time for the examination. It was given by the director of the chemistry department, not the lab teacher.

"The director said, 'Margit Grunbaum. That is a Jewish name! You are that Jewish girl who took that young man's place.'

"I said, 'Yes, there was no other way to learn. Excuse me.'

"'Okay,' he said. 'We will see what you have learned.'

"He began very roughly to ask me questions, difficult questions, but I answered them all very well. Finally he grunted, 'You answered everything correctly, but I will not give you an excellent. I will only write satisfactory here on the paper.'

"He did this because he was an anti-semite," my grandmother explained to me. "You see. This is why it is not so easy to be Jewish. You understand? I was upset but I thought to myself, I don't care. I am here studying to be a doctor. I went to the histology exam and I did very well. I completed my medical studies in Prague and I graduated. But then came a very difficult time. I could not open my own practice because the economy was very bad in Hungary in 1927. No one could afford to see a doctor.

"Later I became a very good doctor, a children's doctor in Russia and then in New York," my grandmother smiled, her thoughts jumping ahead to a better time. "When I came to this country I said to myself, Margit, you can now again be a doctor. For twenty years I had not been able to practice. In Turkey and Venezuela only citizens could be doctors. But I had to study for the exam in this new language, English. I still remember how my dear husband helped me study with flashcards. All the night he was quizzing me. I passed the exam and got a job in a good hospital in New York. I was sixty years old when I began working there and there I worked until I was seventy-five. They liked me very much. It came out all right."

"But what about in Hungary?" I reminded her.

She backtracked. "But in that time in Hungary when I was a young woman just out of medical school I could not come ahead. I was very unhappy. Every day my mother and father were fighting. I was so depressed. I was twenty-seven years old; my father wanted me to marry his accountant. I said I would not marry this man. My mother was very upset and terribly sick with tuberculosis. All the night she was coughing blood. I said I cannot go on this way, living in this house. Every day my mother would ask, 'When will you marry? You have to marry.' I liked young men, but nothing romantic happened. I had an intelligent face, a nice face and we spoke about many things, walking along the Danube, drinking coffee, but they did not ask me to dance. I was too serious, always thinking, no sense of humor. Do you understand?"

I touched her hand gently. I understood exactly.

"Now I have a good humor but then I did not. I was a very serious and sad young woman. I said, I have to do something. I cannot stay here in my father's house. I want a child, I have to marry. I was so desperate feeling.

"So my father and I put an ad in the newspaper. 'Looking for a nice Jewish man, intelligent, professional to marry intelligent, professional woman.'"

She coughed, gave me a long steady look from her black eyes. "Irene, it is not a secret any more. I do not want to have secrets from you. He answered the ad and he came to my parents' house for dinner. He was older than me and an engineer. I thought, I will test this man. I began asking him questions about music, about art, about literature. I asked him about Heinrich Ibsen. He was so good discussing *The Doll's House* with me that I said, this is a very intelligent man. I will marry him. So we married, but there was a complication.

"My husband could not find work in Hungary. In this time, there was no work in Hungary. So he had gone to Greece where they gave him work. He was in Athens where he learned Greek so quickly and so well that they could not believe it. He was very good with languages, my husband. But they said before we give you work you have to convert to be Greek Orthodox. We cannot give a Jew work. He converted. But he did not tell Jakab, my father, who was a very orthodox Jew, the president of the Jewish community in our part of Budapest, about this conversion. We had a beautiful wedding in the Temple. They carried me in a golden carriage with big red horses. I still remember the lacy veil that my mother made trailing behind me in a long train. If my father had known Sandor had converted, was not Jewish anymore . . . *Gott*, I do not know what would have happened."

Margit fingered the tablecloth and was silent for a long moment. Finally she said, "I wish that you my granddaughter had come to better know your grandfather. You know, he was a good man?"

I searched my mind for a good memory of Sandor. "I always liked showing him my photographs before he got sick."

"He liked photography, my husband," my grandmother smiled. "Everywhere we traveled, Turkey, Greece, France, Canada, Venezuela, everywhere he would take photographs."

"Do you still have those photographs?"

"Sure I have them."

"Could I see them someday?"

"Of course. When you are interested, I will show you the photographs by your grandfather. He was a very intelligent and clever man. Sometimes a little harsh, a little bad-tempered, but he loved me very much. He said, 'I only need you. No one else.' But then he got sick. When he turned eighty he said, 'Eighty is the end of life. Now I will die.' Soon he began to forget all the English he knew. He no longer read *The New York Times* and the Hungarian papers he had always studied with so much care each day. He no longer listened to Beethoven and Brahms. He just sat in one blue chair and stared out the window. 'Sandor,' I would say, I was so worried about him. 'What is it? What do you see?'

"'Where am I?' he would ask me.

"Can you imagine? I would answer, 'Sandor, you are with me, your Margit, in your apartment in Yonkers.'

"'What is Yonkers?' he would ask in an angry voice.

"And so it went, worse and worse. Sandor had always done everything financial: stocks, real estate, our bank accounts. Letters from the bank began to stack up on the dining table. Our stock broker called every week wanting to know what choices we would make. I wanted to help but I knew nothing. I had never learned how to balance a checkbook, how to understand these complicated American financial statements.

"One day I decided, I will learn this checking account. I sat down at the table with Sandor. 'Sandor,' I said, 'Tell me everything and I will do this job from now on.'

"Sandor was quiet for a long time. He looked out the window at the leaves falling on the grass. There were many beautiful trees and flowers there, like a park it was. Finally he looked at me. There were tears in his eyes. I had almost never seen my husband cry. 'Margit,' he said, pointing to the top of his head, 'It's empty. I don't remember anything.'

"After that, sometimes he did not even know me. I retired from my job as a doctor. I tried to take care of him and manage, but it was too much. I was almost seventy five myself. Finally, your father had to come on the airplane and take both of us to California. We gave Sandor a pill to calm him down, only a small dose what would not harm him, but still he was so upset. On the plane he cursed us and yelled. I was so afraid. 'Where am I?' he yelled. 'Where are you taking me? Who *are* you?' Had I not had my son to help me, I never would have made it."

What if this happens to Ernie, I thought to myself. What if he stops knowing who he is some day? I pictured Sandor, his thick gray mustache, his bow tie, his shiny bald head. I remembered how as a teenager I would sit next to him in the shade in the backyard and we would examine each photograph together, for composition, lighting, depth of field. He would speak slowly in broken English and I would switch my sentence structure around so he could understand me more easily. "This one you like?" I would ask shyly, wanting the praise of this formal old man, and he would answer, "This one you made very good, yes."

I remembered my grandfather sitting stiffly next to a plate of barbecue, his felt hat and dark suits absurd in the southern California heat, remembered his rough voice upsetting Ernie, telling him what to do with his life. I felt sad, sitting there with my grandmother, remembering Granapu Sandor, realizing how little I really knew about him.

I asked Grananyu what my great-grandmother was like.

"Oh, Regina, your great-grandmother, her writing was like pearls. She gave me a photo of herself when I graduated from medical school. It hangs next to my bed. It's been there for the last fifty years. In writing like pearls she wrote on the photograph, 'I give this photograph to my dear daughter. Part of my life has been your ambition to make a career for yourself as a doctor.'"

Margit leaned forward to touch my red curls, "Her hair was red like yours, only dark red. When you came into the world your red hair was a mystery to your parents. Your father came to me, asking, almost accusing me, 'Who had red hair?' 'Why my mother did, of course,' I said, angry that he had forgotten his grandmother." She touched my hair again, "You have hair like my mother's."

"Was Regina like me in other ways?"

"Yes, she had your passion for learning. She always liked to learn. She secretly studied French and read books in German."

"Why secretly?"

"Because Jakab believed women should not study. My mother burned electric light bulbs like jewels at her evening bedside. Through my bedroom wall I could hear my father swearing at her every night. Always his words were the same, 'Again you read and the electric light is on.'

'I cannot go to sleep if I do not read,' my mother would plead.

'But my electric light costs good money.'"

"*His* electric light?" I sputtered. "Guess he never let her forget who paid the utility bill."

"Yes. He never let her forget this. But she had a secret religion as well," Margit leaned close, almost whispered. "She had a double religion. On Shabbat she burned the candles and said the prayers. Then the next day, Sunday, she read from the Catholic Bible, and said those prayers."

"Really? Did her husband know about this?"

"No! *Gott*, that would have been terrible," my grandmother shuddered. "But I myself also have this double religion. As a child I would go to the big Basilica downtown and pray by a tall column. I felt *Gott* could hear me better there. Today I go to Temple with my friend Magda, and sometimes to church with other friends. Another friend of mine is teaching me about reincarnation."

I was amazed. I had no idea my grandmother was so eclectic. Reincarnation? A double religion? Why did my grandmother and great-grandmother feel the need to turn to Catholicism to talk to God? Maybe it had something to do with Jakab. "Grananyu, why did Regina marry such a difficult man?"

She sighed, her shoulders tensed. I was almost sorry I asked. "When I married she gave me a journal of her life as a young girl. How I wish I hadn't read it. She wrote that she fell in love with a doctor, but her father didn't have enough dowry to satisfy the man's parents, so they wouldn't give their consent for marriage. Her pride was hurt. So she vowed she'd marry a rich man. 'I will show my father. I *will* marry a wealthy man,' were her last words in the journal, and then she wrote no more."

"So my great-grandfather was a rich man?"

"Yes, he was a rich man. But he was also very nervous, a harsh, ambitious man who worked his way from textile apprentice, to textile factory owner. Always he was berating my mother, scolding her. She hated seders because my father would find something wrong with how the plate was arranged, a speck of dust on the dishes, something was always wrong. She used to sit and tremble while he checked to make sure everything was done absolutely correctly. It was not a happy home." Margit was quiet for a long moment, remembering.

"We would walk along the Danube and sit in a beautiful outdoor cafe, have a coffee. Then they would begin to argue. I would say, Again they argue. No one could get along with my father. One by one each of his five brothers tried to work for him in the textile factory. One by one they left. The youngest decided to go to America. 'Look Jakab, you are my brother,' he wrote. 'I want to go to America. Please help me. Please send me money so I can go to America.' What did my father send his brother? A Talmud he sent him! Not money. A Talmud. As if that would do him any good. But he went to America anyway, got a job on a boat so he could pay for his passage. He got to America. Eventually he started a department store in New York."

"Your father sounds like he was a really difficult man, so stubborn."

"Yes. But," she added quickly, "my mother had a good life. She went to the best stores in Budapest for her clothes; she had everything—a maid, a cook, teachers for her children . . ."

"She never had her freedom. Her freedom would have been worth so much more."

My grandmother sighed. "Yes, that was what she wanted for me, freedom. Her greatest wish was for my education. She refused to teach me how to cook or sew. She was afraid these skills would keep me from my profession."

The clock chimed eleven times and we were both quiet, waiting for it to finish. I looked out the window at the foothills. Another smoggy day.

"When I was fifteen my father hit me when my mother was not home. Did you know this?"

"What? He hit you?"

"Yes, I don't remember exactly what happened but I came in the room and said something to him and he hit me in the head. I fainted and fell on the floor. I think I fainted because I was thinking, I am a strong little girl. I will go and attack him. Then I thought to myself, What? Your own father you are going to attack? That made such a terrible storm in me that I fainted. My father called a doctor. The doctor said I had been hysterical."

"Did the doctor know your father had hit you?"

"No, I don't think so. I spent three days in bed. This was a very unhappy home. I wanted to help my dear mother. I told her it would be better for her to leave. So when I was twenty I helped my mother escape on the train to her parents' house in Saraspotak. But my two brothers wrote to my mother, 'Don't leave us alone.' They begged her to come home. She did, even though she was humiliated."

I was amazed, imagining the courage it must have taken for my grandmother to take such a step. Then the pain of watching her mother go back to her father.

"And so it went on. Sometimes I cried. I said how can I live in this home? But I lived there even after my graduation from medical school."

"Couldn't you move out on your own? Or could women do that then?"

"Yes, some women did live on their own, but they had to have money. I had no money to open my own office. Those were hard years in Hungary. Besides," she confessed, "I was not enough bold. I was afraid to go to America. I was afraid to leave home."

My grandmother afraid? I didn't think my grandmother was afraid of anything. "So what happened to your mother when the war started?"

My grandmother's eyes were on the fireplace. A line of carved blue elephants from India marched across the mantelpiece. A Maori mask with green slitted eyes watched us from another wall.

"My mother did not live that long," she finally said. "Times were so bad that my father asked my mother to work in the textile shop, even though she hated sales work. My mother got tuberculosis working in his cold drafty shop. From sanitarium to sanitarium we went in search of a cure. I went with her, because I loved her more than anyone. But she died of tuberculosis at the beginning of the war."

She became silent again for a long moment. The moment held her gently.

"She died in a hospital alone. By then, I had fled Hungary and gone to Turkey with my husband. Do you know how I found out about my mother's death?"

"No."

"I read about it in the newspaper in Turkey. A Hungarian friend said to me, 'I'm so sorry about your mother, that she died.' I said, 'What?' I did not know about it. Can you imagine? Imre had already been deported and my other brother, Joszi, did not write and tell me what happened. My father was not with her either. She died alone. Then my father died too, when the Russians bombed Budapest at the end of the war, not from the bombs themselves, but from fear. A bomb fell. He rushed downstairs into the cellar, had a heart attack."

I tried to imagine finding out my mother had died by reading the newspaper, to imagine bombs falling on her garden, on the house where I live. I can't really imagine any of this—my grandmother's life.

What about my great-great grandmother? What was she like?

"Ethel was a very energetic woman. I remember her voice echoing across the courtyard calling for the servants, for the cow to be milked. Once we were in our carriage and we met an automobile; the horses were frightened. She made the man in the automobile stop, wait for us to pass, even though he was very angry with us."

I liked this idea, cars stopping for horses.

"She used to rise at four a.m. to bake hard *komisz* bread for me on the days I left on the train to go home to Budapest. That kind of bread kept well for train trips. Everyone loved Ethel's cooking. The weddings she cooked for were famous.

"But not only cooking! Ethel was a very intellectual woman, with a desire to learn. I remember my grandmother deciding to learn French at age ninety. She was always reading too, even though she had ten children, four sons and six daughters."

"What about Ethel's husband, your grandfather? What was he like?"

"Ignatz. Ignatz Moskowits. That was your great-great grandfather." Margit remembered, "He made Tokay wine. You know what is Tokay wine?"

"Yes, my father talks about this wine. He says it is a golden flame in a bottle."

"Yes, it is magic! The grapes grow on volcanic hills in northern Hungary. Maybe they catch the fire in the earth. It is a very fine wine. When my grandfather gave wine tours, I used to hide in the cellar behind the wine barrels and watch the tourists spit into a bucket. Do you know why they did this?"

"I went wine tasting once. We saw the buckets people can spit into so they won't get drunk."

"So you know this?" my grandmother beamed, pleased with my worldliness. "My grandfather had one vineyard in town, and one in the hills. He owned a beautiful wood where the family went for picnics. Ignatz studied the Talmud in a Hebrew college. He was not so religious like my father. He liked to have a good time, playing cards with his friends in the village square, gambling for his daughters' dowries."

"Didn't you go back to Saraspotak, Grananyu?"

"Yes, only once, about ten years ago, with your father. I wanted to find the house of my grandparents. My son and I walked up and down the street for hours looking, but we could not find it. I did not have the address. I was getting so upset, so despairing in myself. Then I saw a lawyer's office. I thought, He will know how to find this place. I went into his office to ask if he could help me find this house. He said, 'This makes no problem. My wife will know.' His wife was an expert in the history of this town, and knew exactly where my family had lived. She gave me the address. Immediately we went there. We had walked by this house twice already, but I didn't recognize it. Everything was so changed.

"In my mind it was a huge house with a big drive for a carriage and horses. Now it was a small house on a regular street next to other houses close together. We knocked on the door . . ."

"Wait, you just knocked on the door? Weren't you worried about how you would be received?" I thought of all the awful stories I'd read about survivors going back to their hometowns. They had doors slammed in their faces. Their very presence was a disturbing reminder of the past.

"No. I was not worried. It turned out that the woman who lived there was Jewish, a very distant relative. Can you imagine? After all this time. We went in the house. My son was so embarrassed by me.

"First I asked, 'What happened to all the nice furniture?'

"Then I walked into the garden and asked, 'Where is the cow and the goat? Where is the well?'

"Finally, I asked, 'What happened to the carriage house and the beautiful horses?' The woman told me they had turned the carriage house into a garage. She was very nice and patient. My son was angry with me for asking these questions, so embarrassed."

"And what about Turkey? Why didn't you go with your husband when he left for Turkey?" I asked. "Why did you stay in Hungary even though things were getting so bad?"

"We could not go until he had work. I had a little son, your father," she said. "I was afraid of the Nazis. I tried to tell all my relatives, my uncle, my cousins, everyone, Go to America. Go to London. Go. We cannot stay here! They would not believe me. And they all died. My Uncle Erwin, he made a suicide when he knew the Nazis were coming for him. He gave his wife poison and then he took it himself. Another cousin jumped out of a window. Terrible! After, I felt terrible."

My grandmother looked at me, her eyes damp and magnified by her black-rimmed eyeglasses.

"It wasn't your fault they died. You're not responsible." My grandmother carried this guilt her whole life, that so many family members died, while she lived.

Margit paused, nodded her head. "You are right, my dear, I am not responsible." After a moment she continued, "After one year Sandor sent for me and your father.

"My little son and I arrived in Istanbul late in the evening at the hotel where my husband had made a reservation for us. It was a nice hotel, but there were many young women living there, alone. I think it was," Margit stopped and glanced at me sideways, "you know, a hotel for prostitutes. You know what this is, sure?"

"Of course."

"But it was late and we had to stay. I don't think my husband knew what kind of hotel he had chosen us. I brought my bags upstairs. Then an older woman knocked on my door and asked me if I wanted male company!

"The next morning my son opened the curtains. There was Istanbul, the capital of the Ottoman empire. The bridge over the Golden Horn, bronze hills, narrow streets winding through the city, the blue of the Mediterranean in the distance. Soon there was a knock at the door. There was my dear husband. I was so happy to see him. But after almost a whole year apart my little son did not recognize his father. We got on the train and traveled to Ankara, where we were to live. I was shocked by the sandstone mountains outside the train window, barren, depressing. What was this place where we had come to live?

"The train arrived in Ankara. We took a cab to the apartment my husband had rented. It had no central heat, only a small wood stove in one room, and no refrigerator. We had to buy our food fresh every day, except during the winter when I kept the milk in an ice box hanging on the balcony. But the streets were bright with flowers planted everywhere.

"I walked through the streets of Ankara, in my new home, this Middle Eastern country. The women wore long dark dresses. Their faces were covered by veils. The men smoked long pipes comfortably in coffee houses all day. Some were smoking opium. Women did not enter the coffeehouses; they only went out of the house to shop for lamb meat, vegetables, baklava, and the strong liquor, raki."

"Was it hot in Turkey?"

"In the summer it was very hot. In winter there was snow. In Turkey I became very good friends with my neighbors, like I do everywhere." She paused. "Irene, do you make friends?"

"Yes. Many friends."

"And these friends, are they women or do you have male friends too?"

"Mostly women."

My grandmother's black eyes zeroed in on me. "Mostly women. You must have both man and woman friends." She reached across the table and touched my cheek.

"Your hand feels cold. Are you cold?"

"No, only a little arthritis. My hands feel cold during the day and then during the night they are so burning." She saw my concerned face. "This makes nothing, don't worry. Everything will be all right. I am my own doctor. I take cod liver oil and vitamins."

"Okay. Tell me more about your friends in Turkey."

"I spoke French, and educated women all spoke French. So we had good conversations, drank strong Turkish coffee in their homes. Some holidays I visited seven or eight friends, drank coffee with each one. You can imagine how I felt by the evening. Many of them told me about being in harems when they were younger. My husband would stay home. He said he did not need friends.

"Meanwhile, my little son was in a French boarding school in Istanbul. I did not want him so far away. But my husband said that he would there get the best education, with the Jesuits. Every week I would send him a package of my Hungarian walnut pastry. He wrote that he missed me. I was so afraid for him when the Germans almost invaded Turkey. My husband sent for him in the middle of the night. I made him such reproaches, that our little son was in danger and so far from us. But everything came out all right. Now life is good." She looked at me, almost pleading. "We have not to think so much of the past."

But I couldn't stop asking questions. I was afraid my grandmother would die and I would still have questions. "What did you do in Turkey? You couldn't be a doctor."

"No, I could not be a doctor," she sighed. "I could only be a doctor if I became a Turkish citizen, and we knew we could not become citizens if we ever hoped to come to the United States. That was our dream, to come to America. I could not practice medicine. Really Irene, I was not too happy. I painted some, and visited the women with their coffee, listened to their stories about the harems."

So, my grandparents had wanted all along to come to the United States. I thought about the odds against me sitting there. What if they'd stayed in Turkey? "Grananyu, why did you leave?"

"We had to leave. The last few months were terrible. They began persecuting the Armenians and the Jews. A Hungarian showed pictures of Ankara to some friends when he visited Hungary, and that was it. They said all Hungarians had to leave; we were spies. My Turkish women friends stopped talking to me. We fled for Italy on a boat."

"Irene, I want to tell you about my brother, Imre. He was very much like your brother, Jeffrey."

"What happened to him?"

There was a pause. In the silence I could hear the metallic ticking of the grandfather clock on top of the cabinet. Grananyu's face twisted and she fingered her tea cup. She took a long drink, then set down her cup and turned to address me.

"What happened? I will tell you what happened. It is okay to tell you now. You must know these things. It is not a secret," she said, perhaps to herself. "I loved my little brother Imre very much. He was a very interesting young man and so handsome all the girls wished they could dance with him. He played the violin like so a Gypsy, so gay. He could sing too. When I left Hungary for Turkey on the train right before the war broke out he accompanied me for one long station stop. That was sixty miles. All the way he was singing to me, one Hungarian melody after another, in a beautiful baritone voice.

"And then . . ." She stopped talking and looked out into the valley, as if the past itself lived out there somewhere beyond the freeway, "then when I got to Turkey they wrote me. He had disappeared. He was a very uncompromising young man, a man with a conscience. When the Nazis came for him they said if he converted they would not take him. He refused. He said, Never. I am Jewish and I will stay Jewish. They took him. He should not have said this. They took him! The Nazis. He disappeared. You understand?" Margit asked, her voice suddenly shrill.

I'd heard this story before but it still made my hands sweat. The words sped through my brain like a train, faster and faster. Disappeared. Nazis. Disappeared. Breathless, I couldn't speak for a minute. Finally I managed, "Yes, I understand. But you got out of Hungary. You got out. How come you survived and Imre didn't?"

"I had to convert. I had to convert to get out of Hungary and be accepted into Turkey. Sandor insisted that I had to convert to Catholicism before I left Hungary, otherwise I would not make it through Serbia and Bulgaria. He was right. In Zagreb, the capital of Serbia, they took me off the train and examined my Aryan documents very closely. Had I not converted they would not have let me through. I took a three-week class in Catholicism from a priest. My cheeks burned. I was so upset. Can you imagine? I was so weeping, that the priest said to me, he knew why I was there, 'Don't be so upset. The Christian religion is the continuation from the Jewish religion.' He was right. I converted and I was baptized in the Basilica. But I never have forgotten my dear little brother who would not convert. They killed him. Now do you understand why we had to hide who we were?" My grandmother stopped talking, took off her thick glasses, and wiped them on her blouse. She looked at me, "My dear, you must be very careful who you tell that you are Jewish. It can bring suffering."

"But I am happy to be Jewish. I want to know everything."

"You can know it. But do not so boldly say, *I am a Jew.* It is very bold to say this. And you must remember, you are equal. A Jew can do anything. You are the equal of everyone."

The next morning we went for a walk through the suburban neighborhood. "Look at those white flowers," my grandmother pointed, "They have a beautiful shape, like a musical instrument. Can you not see it?"

"Yes," I smiled. "Like trumpets."

"What has the name this flower?"

"Calla lilies."

"Calla lilies," my grandmother repeated slowly. "That is a beautiful name. I like this! Look at those other flowers, the purple ones next to the lilies. Such colors together I would like to paint."

"Those are azaleas," I said proudly.

"You know these flowers?" Grananyu looked up at me and smiled. "You are a smart woman, my granddaughter."

Small children pedaled their tricycles up and down the sidewalk. "Take care," Margit warned, steering me away from them. I helped her down the steeper curbs when we crossed side streets.

"You help me so much, Irene," my grandmother said. "You are a very kind young woman." She stopped in her tracks, quiet for a moment, held her head to one side. Then she continued.

"Not so young anymore. When I was your age I already was married and had a child." She stopped and looked up at me. I felt like a giant next to her. My father always said it drove him crazy, when Margit kept stopping each time she had a new thought. A lawn sprinkler hissed behind us.

"But you have made many accomplishments. Working in a library—that is a very fine job. Only you have to be less serious," she admonished me. "You must enjoy life."

We walked a little further down the road to a small park with swings and a sandbox. My grandmother lowered herself down slowly onto a park bench and sat on the edge, feet dangling. She was quiet for a minute. I looked down at our feet together on the grass, my running shoes next to her beige loafers. Then I spotted a hole in her left shoe, near her toe.

"Grananyu," I pointed. "There's a hole in your shoe."

She looked down. "That makes nothing," she said. "These are very fine, expensive shoes. My husband bought them for me in New York."

"Grananyu," I said carefully, not wanting to hurt her feelings. "They are beautiful shoes, but doesn't the hole bother you?"

"Now you sound like my son: 'Anyu get some new shoes, a new sweater,' he is always saying. I tell him, 'Why should I get new ones? These are fine clothes. Clothes cost good money. Besides, I am 94. I have not many years left on this earth. Why should I buy new shoes?'"

I didn't like thinking about my grandmother being so old. I was quiet, counting the dandelions in the grass. I lost count. There must have been at least one for each year my grandmother had lived.

"Shoes are not important. What is important is being here with you, my granddaughter. Tell me, what will you do with this interview from your Grananyu, with these stories I tell you of my life?"

I put my hand on my grandmother's arm. It felt strong and muscular under her silky purple blouse.

"I know I need to hear them. Maybe Jeffrey will want to hear them too. When your great-grandson Mark grows older he can hear them. And I will also write about you," I said softly. "I want you to be remembered."

"That would be good," she mused. "To be remembered by my grandchildren and my great-grandchildren. You know, sometimes I worry that I'll just disappear. Not be Jewish. Not be a doctor. Not be anything at all. It is a terrible feeling that comes over me then."

In June of 1996, the last June of my grandmother's life, she lay in her bed in a residential care home in Arizona, warm pine-scented air blowing in through the open window. I'd traveled hundreds of miles by airplane to see her. I knew Grananyu's heart was failing. I knew this might be our last time together. "I'm just so tired," she kept saying. "I am always tired." After a while, my father and stepmother offered to leave the room for a few moments to give us time alone.

My grandmother rose on her pillow and turned to me. "You are my everything," she told me.

I swallowed. "You are my everything too," I answered, touching my heart.

"I want to give you life," she said.

I took her tiny ninety-five year-old hand in mine. "See my hands are small, like yours." I held my palm up against hers, measuring the difference, almost like children do. "Your hands are like mine. It's because you gave me life."

"Yes," she said slowly. "I only want that you love me as I love you."

"Of course I love you," I said. I felt numb. I concentrated on storing this conversation away for later, on not giving in to my tears. Outside the room, someone was talking about chicken and mashed potatoes for dinner. I got up and retrieved my grandmother's water glass from the table by her bed, and held it for her as she drank deeply through a straw. Then she lay back and studied me silently for awhile through dark, serious eyes. "It is good to look upon your beautiful face," she said finally. "I think you love life. This love is the most important thing. Love, to be optimistic, and to have a good sense of humor. Without a sense of humor, I would have died."

The next month, my father, my brother and I cleaned out my grandmother's condo in LeisureWest. She was too sick to ever live there again, in fact, she was dying. The official diagnosis was congestive heart failure, but my grandmother said her body was just worn out. It looked like the 19th century in that condo. I obsessed about wanting her gold Victorian couch. My grandmother lay on that couch every afternoon to nap. We always sat on it to talk. I couldn't stand the idea of it going to the Goodwill. How could I transport it hundreds of miles north to my house in Santa Cruz? Then I looked at the couch as if seeing it for the first time. It was old, faded, stained. Why hadn't I ever noticed that before?

There were houseplants that needed water and old Oriental carpets that were ragged around the edges. Who would want them? There were cracked white china plates and pots with lids that did not match. There was a file box with addresses on scraps of paper, a clock that chimed but was difficult to wind, requiring a push and shove from my father every other month. There were two narrow, ancient, single beds and the chair that my grandfather was dying in so long ago. There were boxes and boxes of old chocolate in the sideboard, a little sweetness. Her pantry shelves were sticky with honey.

I sat on the couch and felt lost. What would I do when my grandmother died?

"We should just throw this out," my father said. We were in the study by then, cleaning out my grandmother's desk. We had already emptied the heavy wooden drawers of their burden of canceled checks, fundraising appeals from Haddasah, her opera glasses, boxes of unused Christmas cards without envelopes.

He held a small book in the palm of his hand, leather-bound, with red leaves. "Let me see," I begged, and we stopped for a minute to examine the mysterious little book. "Mirjam" it said on the cover in small gold capitals, a spray of gold stars arcing above the letters. I could not read the Hungarian introduction but on page 4 the author, Dr. Kiss Arnold, signed the text with the inscription: "Budapest, 1909, Februar 2." I turned to the back and read the table of contents. Even though it was in Hungarian I could make out the words: "*Kol Nidré, Peszach, Szukkoth, Chanuka.*"

"Hey, it's a prayer book," I said to my father. "We can't throw this out!"

"Oh, Irene. Do you really want this? You can't even read it."

"Sure I want it," I said, clutching the little Hungarian prayer book, glaring at him.

"Okay, okay, Irene," he sighed. I took the little book home with me to Santa Cruz, where it perches on my shelf like a question mark. Was this my grandmother's prayer book? Perhaps it was my great-grandmother Regina's? With a publication date of 1909 it is old enough to have been Regina's. But did either of them really use it? It's in almost mint condition, the pages crisp, not well-thumbed like I'd imagine a prayer book to be. Who was Dr. Kiss Arnold? Does the title "Mirjam" mean it is a woman's prayer book?

This prayer book sits on my shelf and I treasure it because it is the only religious Jewish family object that has been passed down to me. I like to think of Margit or Regina's hands holding it, their voices raised in song.

The last time I visited my grandmother, a week before her death, her black eyes only recognized me once. She blew me kisses and said: "Irene! Irene! Irene!"

I held her bony hand lightly, afraid it would break. My own hand was sweaty. I offered her water but she turned her head away. My neck ached. English had left her. I tried to speak to her in my few words of German, which was her second language after Hungarian. *"Ich liebe dich,"* I love you, I whispered. *"Trinken." "Essen,"* I urged her to eat and drink, but she seemed not to hear. She would not even take her medicine.

I could not cry. My father and I climbed mountains, trying to escape what was happening to my grandmother's body. I ate omelets. I ran eight miles along a ridge at sunrise. We had Christmas turkey—all as my grandmother lay panting.

Two days before she died, Margit stopped eating and drinking. When my father tried to coax her to take her medicine in a little yogurt she refused. He sat her gently up in bed so she faced him. "Anyu, if you don't take your medicine you will die," he said. Her eyes got large. She looked straight at him and said calmly, "I want to die." It was a relief and inspiration to me to know that she made such a conscious and courageous decision to let go of her life.

IV.

GRIEF SOUP

Grananyu and Irene about 1972

The night my grandmother died, I dreamed of a huge pot of black bean soup. I kept dipping bowls of soup out of the pot, but it kept refilling itself to its original level. I said to myself in the dream, My grief is as deep and bottomless as that soup.

My father stood in front of the open grave at Pacific View Cemetery in Newport Beach. There were olive trees and elm trees. He recited the lessons his mother taught him: Fit in but don't get pushed around. Be somebody! Don't be a nobody. I read a poem for my grandmother. Later, the rabbi asked me if I was a writer. My brother said a prayer which contained the unmentionable word in our family: God.

Next to my grandmother's grave lay my grandfather. Someday my father will be buried there, too. Nineteen years ago I stood on the lawn above the Pacific, heard the Kaddish for the first time. A veil parted, revealing my family's history to me.

Now an orange backhoe buried my grandmother while we all stood there silently. Only my nine-year-old nephew cried: "Granny nu! Granny nu!" Afterwards, our scattered and divorced family gathered to eat and talk. Zachertorte from Safeway. Turkey and pastrami sandwiches. We drove the long freeway north.

Eleven months after my grandmother's death I fall in love with Lori, the woman I am to marry. She tells me my grandmother has one year after her death to travel into the other world, the world of light. The way mourners help the dead make that journey is to say the Kaddish, the Jewish prayer for the dead.

Lori and I sit on her bed. We are not a traditional minyan. We are two women who love each other. Lori finds the words for the Kaddish. We sit close together. One of my hands rests on her warm shoulder. In her gentle voice she chants—*Yit-ga-dal ve-yit-ka-dash sh-may ra-ba be-al ma di-ve-ra.*

I say the ancient Aramaic syllables. After one stanza, I stop. Is that blood roaring in my ears, or the wind? I drop my head. Lori's voice, her shoulder, are all that keep me from flying out the window behind us. Where is my grandmother?

When Lori and I said Kaddish that first fall we were together I closed my eyes and saw a movie of Jewish history—pyramids, and shtetls swirling in a continuous loop. When we said Kaddish, Lori's head relaxed. She closed her dark blue eyes as if she was in a trance. When we said Kaddish, I felt someone, not Lori, lightly touch the right side of my head, then my left hand. The hand got warm. A vein stood out.

Ritual is a kind of intimacy, like making love. Lori said she was falling in love with me. When we made love, I felt for the first time that it was okay to touch a woman, that all my passion and feeling were welcome.

Ritual is a kind of intimacy, like making love. Or is making love a kind of ritual?

My father called me on October 29 that year. It was his mother's birthday, only she was dead.

"It was a hard day for me," he confided. "I did a few things to remember her. The Jewish people have a custom, I think it's called *shiva,* in which you close all the windows and the doors and cover them. So I did that. I brought all the statues that were hers to a table in the living room. I went out and bought a beautiful big azalea in a pot, the way she would have liked. I put it on the table. I sat there all day in front of that table and didn't eat anything. I thought about her."

JANUARY 6, 1998

DEAR GRANANYU,

I cut my hair this year and now, with sunglasses on, my mother says I look like you. I think my hair has the same waves yours always did. I thought yours looked elegant; maybe mine is, too?

I honored your *yahrtzheit* tonight. Lori came over to help me. She stepped into my house and her wild, rich, brown curls were loose under that wonderful purple yarmulke, the one that makes her look like a queen. She came in, and I was ready for her.

The hearth was spread with that lavender linen tablecloth you used on your mahogany dining room table. On top of the cloth I had placed mementos of your life—the peacock statues that adorned the top of your china cabinet, some of your doilies. I knew you'd want something royal blue. A weaving from Guatemala. You always loved that shade of blue.

What else? A picture of your mother, whom you loved so much, sitting on the small table that used to rest by your door, where you would put your keys and your purse. That

picture of you and me together, when I was eleven. You are
smiling that warm toothy smile you had when you were
truly happy, unconscious of your buck teeth. You didn't
always smile this way. Mostly you smiled demurely, with
your mouth shut tight, to hide the teeth. As do I. Last week
Lori told me that my full toothy smile is beautiful. I laughed
at her and then I cried a little, because she asked, "When your
grandmother smiled you thought she was beautiful?" I had
to say yes. "So," she said in that wise way she has, "How
come you think her full smile is beautiful, but you don't
think your smile is?" "Touché," I said.

In that photograph of us, I am blinking in bright
southern California sunshine, my bare arms washed out. I
am wearing an orange sleeveless shift, with bright red
flowers on it. Your face is handsome. You have just become
old, your hair already white in waves; you must be in your
early seventies. How warmly you look at the camera. It must
be your son you are looking at, who took the picture. We are
seated on the back steps to the porch, next to the brick walls
of the house that never fell down in the earthquake we
always lived in fear of. Your glasses are around your neck. I
am wearing an embroidered headband and braces on my
teeth. Your arm is draped around my shoulders. I lean
against your breast. We are both wearing stretch pants. I
remember how much I hated those stretch pants that stuck to
my legs in the summer heat. You are wearing the same navy
blue pants you owned twenty years later, and probably the
same black sandals. It is another smoggy day.

I think I remember the day that my father took that
picture. I was shy and didn't want to sit on those stairs with

you. Now, almost thirty years later, you are dead and I am still alive; my teeth still stick out and are crooked because the braces didn't work. I wouldn't be caught dead in an orange shift with red flowers on it. But I still love the picture of us which hangs on my wall.

Tonight was your *yahrtzheit*. Tonight was the night to help you move into the other world. Tonight was the night to let you go. I know you've hung around this entire year, curled into my chest somewhere, cherished and warm. I've suspected you even played a little with my life this year, helping me meet lovers, making special appearances. I've felt you with me when I admired shades of deep blue and purple, when I saw that lilac shirt I would have bought you for your birthday. I felt you with me last week when I stood with your son on a balcony overlooking the Sea of Cortez. I knew how you would have liked to have painted the coast of Baja California, sheathed in golden sunrise, across the water. I knew you would have liked it that my father and I were standing there together, thinking of you. I thought of your love of detail. I thought of your love. I felt your blessings for this precious, growing love between Lori and I, my lover who loves to dance.

Your paintings are all over this house, my gallery by the sea, and my friends admire them. I know you would have liked that. You embodied the marriage of emotion and intellect, of science and art, of oppression and elation. Lori and I sat on the floor, on the Persian rug I inherited from you. The hearth was behind us. Lori led me on a breathing meditation. "Close your eyes," she began. "Feel your breath moving in and out of your body, feel it travel all the way up from your belly, to your heart." I took a deep breath and it shuddered inside of me; my legs began to shake. "Now feel your heart and feel your grandmother touching your heart," Lori said. My eyes were closed. In my mind I saw you reach for my hand. "Now picture your grandmother touching your heart, still touching your heart, but further away, away up in the stars."

I cried. I was still holding onto your hand, but suddenly things were changing. Your arm was growing longer and longer. Suddenly it was a cord and you were floating up through the skylight above me, then up, up into the heavens. I felt your presence leave my heart, and I felt a great grief, the grief I never felt when you died. You were truly gone.

Then we said the Kaddish. We began with the Aramaic, and Lori said it extra slow for me. I've said those words before, but this time each syllable was like extracting a tooth, or breathing under water. Halfway through I broke down and wept, but I forced myself to finish, because I knew those words formed the bridge for your passage. I said the English alone. I was weeping openly and loudly as I did, lamenting, and when I finished I knew I had truly mourned you.

love,

Irene

WHO WILL REMEMBER?

Now that my grandmother is dead, who will remember her? Who will remember these ancestors she spoke about so often to me? Why is it important that they be remembered? Is it because they were citizens of another world, a Hungarian Jewish culture that flourished before the Holocaust, and therefore they provide a doorway into that decimated world? Is this some personal need of mine, some quirk, this remembering, a way of making up somehow for my loss of heritage? Few of my friends know the names of their great-grandmothers, never mind the details of their lives. Perhaps it is this terrible rootlessness of the Anglo-American culture that surrounds me, which renders as strange my passion for remembering and telling the stories of my ancestors. This is a culture of amnesia, even for family history.

I want to remember my great-grandmother Regina Moskowits Grunbaum. I am sitting at this desk, writing, looking at a picture of Regina. Regina is seated at a table in a cafe, close to another woman, whose name has been lost to history. She's dressed all in black, my great-grandmother, and she's wearing a black hat rakishly tilted to one side. She is looking directly at the camera, at me, her dark eyes and handsome features reminding me of the faces of a number of strong women I have loved. A tall glass of tea is in front of her, almost empty. Her friend is sitting very close to her, so close their bodies are touching. Her friend is not looking at the camera. Her glass of tea is farther away, as if she had forgotten it completely. She is looking adoringly at Regina. Her face is slightly behind Regina's, her eyes are fixed on Regina's neck and she is smiling what I can only describe as a flirtatious smile, as if she were about to kiss the back of Regina's neck, or maybe I only want to see it that way. There are roses on the table in front of Regina's friend, white roses, and the friend is dressed in a flowery dress, her hair coifed, lipstick coloring her full lips, contrasting with Regina's black dress and unadorned face. They look so butch and femme. But is that just what I want to see, to believe my great-grandmother Regina might have loved a woman? On the back of the photograph are the words: "1940 jul." That would have been very close to the end of Regina's life, and yet in the picture she does not look sick. She must have been in her sixties. What is the real story of this photograph?

I want to remember Imre, brother of my grandmother. Imre, you were born in 1909, nine years younger than my grandmother. You were a dark, short, athletic man with a deep baritone voice. My grandmother told me that the Nazis said they would send you to a concentration camp unless you converted to Christianity. Your answer was, Never!

NEVER! How did you say this and what was the context? Was it in some petty bureaucrat's office? Was it in some Nazi prison, under torture? Did you know what you were saying, Imre, what the consequences would be? How did my grandmother know you said this word—Never? Where did you die? My grandmother just told me, "they took him and he disappeared." Should I try to trace you all these years later, find out what camp or field you died in. Did you say, Never! because you were religious? Was it just because you were stubborn, like so many members of my family?

Never. Never look back. Look ahead. That was one of my grandmother Margit's sayings. But here I sit at this desk in Santa Cruz, California, thousands of miles and almost sixty years between Imre and me. I am looking back. Will I become a pillar of salt? Will I break into a thousand pieces, fall apart, Imre?

I have thought of you a hundred times, Imre, ever since my grandmother told me your story. She told me you looked like my brother Jeffrey. I have looked into Jeffrey's dark eyes and wondered if he carries your secret. I think of you when I decide not to pass as straight, when I call myself dyke, when I hold my lover's hand, when I publish another book with both my name and the word lesbian on the cover. I think of you when I choose to call myself, "Jew," when I call myself a daughter of Holocaust refugees. Yet, what would you have thought of me? Nine years younger than my grandmother, I could have known you, had dinner with you a thousand times, spilled milk on your lap as a child, heard your songs myself. What would you have thought of me, a dyke with an athletic walk, a woman who dares to live without men, who dares to live alone. Would you have hated me, or been proud of me?

V.

FÖLDÖNFUTO, THE WANDERER:

MY FATHER'S STORY

My father, Regina (left) and Grananyu Margit

"I knew that all behind me was dust and cinders, the past solidified
into bitter salt . . . Now I do not belong anywhere, everywhere a
stranger and at best, a guest."

—Stefan Zweig

LOS ANGELES, 1993

I didn't want to be on that train to the city of my childhood. I hated Los Angeles. I hated the approach through the valley, the long, gray San Fernando Valley, flat and choked with Spanish-style tract houses: fake stucco walls and pink tile roofs the color of the retainer I wore in sixth grade. I hated the malls—the big malls and the mini malls, the stores that repeated themselves: Big 5, Sears, Shop n' Save; Von's, Kmart, Mervyn's, Burger King; Woolworths, WaldenBooks, KFC; 31 Flavors, Taco Bell, Nordstroms. Big 5 . . .

I hated how big the valley was. So big that I felt lost in my father's white Buick, lost on the 134, the 210, the 5, the 101, the 405. Or even on the Amtrak, where I was that night. In the dark the cities blended in a blur of light.

Glendale. It was time to get off. My father was waiting for me outside the adobe train station painted with murals during the WPA days, one of the few adobes that hadn't succumbed to an earthquake. Maybe they'd restored it to look old. It's hard to tell in Los Angeles.

My father tried to hug me, but when he put his arm around my shoulders, and said, "I'm so glad to see you," I stiffened.

Ernie recoiled slightly. "Here, let me take that," he insisted, plucking the backpack out of my hand. I call my father Ernie, ever since the year of the divorce, when my mother asked Jeffrey and me to call her Claire.

"Still carrying the backpack?"

"Hey, it's a lot better for my back than any stupid suitcase," I retorted, instantly slipping into my teenage voice.

"Come on," Ernie said. "We waited for dinner for you. Terry's at home microwaving the meatballs."

I was touched that they'd waited for dinner even though I was two hours late. We got into his sedan and sped up the on-ramp to the freeway, joined thousands of other cars moving at ten miles an hour through the darkness. I shielded my eyes from all the lights. "How do you stand Los Angeles?" I asked.

"I think about leaving, but where would I go? I've lived here longer than anywhere else," he said, as we traversed a high overpass toward another freeway. Please don't let there be an earthquake now, I prayed. I wanted to beg my father, "Leave. Get out, before you die of lung cancer from the smog, lose your soul on the 134, before the whole place collapses in the Big Earthquake that's been overdue for years."

"But Ernie, does this place feel like home?"

"No place feels like home."

I was surprised by Ernie's flat honesty. I again felt the impulse to try and comfort my father, but I didn't know how to begin.

We exited the freeway and passed a shopping center, drove up a hill to a Spanish-style building converted to condos in the early 1980s. Ernie opened the electric gate to the garage with a special coded card. We drove underground, parked next to an oil puddle. I followed my father up a flight of concrete stairs, past the pool landscaped with orange begonias and enormous hibiscus, up another flight of stairs and down a long blue corridor. White lamps with gargoyle faces beamed down at us sweetly. A Muzak version of Mozart, or was it Beethoven, pacified us in the hallway.

A door like every other door, the number painted on it in black italics. I hoped I wouldn't have to find my way back by myself this visit. Last time I came to visit Ernie, I decided to use the exercise room, and it took me twenty minutes to find his apartment afterwards. I kept walking up and down the halls, lost. A woman in pink thongs found me by the elevator, took pity on me and walked me back to my father's apartment. I felt as if I were six years old.

Margit got lost here too. She didn't have much sense of direction either. Maybe she lived so many places she didn't know where she was any more. She said her whole life she'd had a dream about trying to find something she lost.

Ernie opened the door and Terry hugged me. I didn't resist her soft hug. Her eyes were tired, but she looked pretty in the green silk vest she bought last time she and Ernie visited me. She showed me to the guest bedroom and then stepped to the window, pointed across the valley at the next ridge.

"Last week," she said in her calm Iowa way, "I saw a coyote up there on that ridge above the freeway. He stood there for a long time and I watched him. I can hear them sometimes at night, howling up on that hill. People say the coyotes are coming down from the mountains because of the drought. They're drinking out of swimming pools, eating house cats."

I looked across the valley, hoping to glimpse the coyote before the sun plummeted into the smog and painted a poisonous orange sunset. All I could see was dusty oleander, tall scraggly eucalyptus, a murky valley with unidentifiable scrub buried in its gray depths, and the freeway cutting through the hills, as some river might have, long ago.

The three of us sat down to eat.

"These meatballs are good, Ernie."

"My specialty. Make them every Friday."

After dinner, my father and I sat on the couch drinking mint tea. "So you want to hear about my life, Irene. Okay, fire away."

I dove in quickly before Ernie could have second thoughts about this conversation. I had written my father and asked if I could interview him about his life, sent him a list of questions. I'll start with something neutral, I thought. "Ernie, tell me about Venezuela. Why did you go there?"

"It was the only place that would take us. There we were, thrown out of Turkey, stuck in Italy in 1948, stateless, a family without a country. Every day my father would go from consul to consul, trying to get us in somewhere. We wanted to go to the United States, but everyone wanted to come here. It was impossible to get a visa.

"Finally, one day my father came home looking relieved. 'The Venezuelan consul will give me a job in Caracas as an engineer. We will go there.' So again we were going to move. We had already been in Hungary, then Russia, then Turkey for ten years. And I was only seventeen.

"Venezuela, I thought to myself. I don't know anything about it. I went to the library in Rome and read a book. The book said it was a Western-style country, rich with oil and cattle, in many ways dependent on the United States.

"My parents sold everything we owned in order to have enough money for the boat trip. . ."

"How long was the boat trip?"

"Seventeen days. All the way we studied Spanish from a little book. I met a nice Venezuelan girl named Nuria on the boat, and she was teaching me, too. She was a cutie. But when we got to Puerto Cabello I had to say goodbye to her.

"We got there on Good Friday and they wouldn't even let us off the boat because it was such a big religious holiday. Venezuela is a very Catholic country. We sat in the harbor for a whole day."

"Where did you go once the boat stopped?"

"Well, the consul met us at the dock. He'd told my father he'd be in Venezuela himself at that time and he'd come pick us up and drive us from the port to Caracas. All the way across the ocean my father worried about this man keeping his word, how we were going to get to Caracas once we arrived at the port, whether there would really be a job for him. He was so nervous. Such a worrier! He yelled at my mother and me every day. One day he called me a bag of shit." My father took another sip of tea, cleared his throat.

"But we arrived in Caracas and the consul was there. He kept his word. He drove us through the high mountains on a twisty, narrow road. Drivers speeding down the mountain kept crossing the line, aiming straight at us, cursing in Spanish. Well, we couldn't understand them, but we knew they were cursing. Below us, tiny deep valleys glowed in the sun against the dark peaks. Along the road I saw little white crosses, some with fresh flowers on them. Later, we found out the crosses were monuments to people who died in car accidents at those exact spots.

"We arrived in Caracas and went to a little hotel. Boy, were we exhausted! We collapsed into our beds. We were awakened at dawn by a street musician playing a melody about love on his violin. It sounded pretty bad. My father raged about the violinist. But my mother said, 'How beautiful. A country that has music can not be bad.' That's how they always were: my mother the optimist, my father the pessimist. Can you imagine being caught between these two people?

"Anyway, that morning my father said to me, 'Okay, enough loafing. You have to go out and find a job.'"

"But you'd only been there one day."

"You bet. I was exhausted from the long boat trip, disoriented. I could only speak what Spanish I had learned from that little book, and from Nuria. But my father claimed we had no money. I had to go to work, find a job.

"What could I do? I went out and walked the crowded streets of Caracas all day, up and down. It was only April, but it was already boiling hot. Finally I got up my courage and walked into a car mechanic shop. I told the guy I knew how to repair American cars. He hired me, but it wasn't true that I knew about cars. I only knew a little. I was faking it. At the end of the day he said, 'I am sorry. You are a nice young man but I cannot hire you.' I had to go home to my father without a job. And boy, was he pissed.

"The next day I got up and roamed the streets again, and the next day and the next. Finally, I got a job working for Union Cash Register. They taught me how to repair cash registers. At first, while my Spanish was not so good, I only worked inside the shop doing repairs. As my Spanish got better, I began going to stores and selling the cash registers to business people.

"One day I picked up the phone at the shop. A man from a large business said he needed one hundred cash registers. They knew they wanted to buy them already, just needed someone to come out and do the paperwork, arrange for the delivery. I couldn't believe my good luck. We salesmen were paid a commission on each cash register we sold. This would mean a huge amount of money for me. I went out and sold the cash registers. Then I went to the manager and asked, 'Where's my commission?'

"The manager replied, 'Ernesto,' they called me Ernesto there, 'you know that commission is for selling cash registers, not just for doing paperwork. Those cash registers were already sold before you even got there.'

"'But it said on my contract that I would get a commission for all the cash registers I sold! My name is on the sales slip. I should get the money.' I insisted. The manager got really mad and refused to give me the money. So I wrote to the headquarters of Union Cash Register in the United States and explained what happened. They wrote back and said the manager had to give me the money. That's the money I went to engineering school with. My father had no money to give me, so I was very happy because I really wanted to be an engineer."

I picked up my cup of cold tea, looked at my father sitting next to me on the couch. I remembered being a teenage girl, refusing to meet his eyes at the breakfast table, drinking my orange juice made from concentrate, eating my soft-boiled egg, with eyes only for my mother. He was dangerous to me then, a scary, formal man who said I had no right to my own opinions, no right to contradict him.

Why am I still afraid of Ernie, I thought. He's not trying to control my life anymore. I looked at my father in his polo shirt and gold-rimmed glasses, staying up late to spend precious time with his daughter, to tell me stories. This was the first time he'd told me these stories in such detail. He was just a man who was caught somewhere between Hungary and America, between Venezuela and Turkey, and got a little lost.

I took a big breath and asked the question I'd been wanting to ask him for over half my life: "Ernie, why did you and Claire decide not to tell my brother and me that you were Jewish?"

My father spoke carefully, in his methodical, engineer's style, looking directly at me. He said in his lightly Hungarian-accented voice:

"Our main intention in deciding not to tell you we were Jewish, your mother's and mine, was to shield you: To shield you from discrimination; to shield you from being associated with people who are discriminated against; to shield you from internal problems in your own mind—who am I?"

I was startled by the irony in this statement. I have spent over half my life pondering the meaning of my Jewish identity, wondering exactly that—*who am I?* If my parents had not hidden my Jewishness from me would I have given the matter much thought at all? Did their very attempts to "protect" me stimulate the curiosity which led me on the journey that now strips away the shields they had wanted to bequeath me? He continued:

"What is Jewishness? Jewishness is a religion, not an ethnicity. There are Polish Jews, Hungarian Jews, Russian Jews, American Jews. I'm not quite comfortable with the concept of Jewishness being a race, although there is such a thing as a racial characteristic. It's more a cultural thing. That can be changed. Culture can be changed. Race can't be changed very easily. It takes many generations to change that.

"I don't subscribe to the deterministic view that once Jewish always Jewish, because there are lot of other influences that are much more powerful. When a Jew and a non-Jew marry, is the child Jewish or non-Jewish? Jews would like to say it is Jewish because they're trying to preserve that cultural identity.

"I think the Jews create their own enclave. That, of course, creates resentment in the outside community, because they single themselves out and claim to be better than everybody else. Because to preserve their identity, to avoid being assimilated by the majority, they created their own enclaves, married only Jewish people. You know for a Jew to marry a non-Jew is one of the biggest sins in the world. The non-Jews know that. Whether right or wrong, some of the anti-semitism is the fault of the Jewish nation.

"The other thing is that they engaged in fields that create resentment. When you're a moneylender, the typical Jewish moneylender, nobody likes you, because they owe you something and you want it back, you want to be paid, and they don't have the resources to pay you. So now you're foreclosing on him, taking his home away, taking his business away, because he hasn't paid yet. Is that going to create goodwill? Obviously not. So there's a lot of anger there. The Jews created an environment where their activities were not appreciated by the other population. They were more intelligent. They became college professors and things like that. These are the very things that my mother considers to be the outstanding characteristics of Jews. They are intellectuals. But it caused also some of the problems that then resulted in the pogroms and the Holocaust and all that. I'm not saying it's all their fault. Obviously not. But it contributed to the fire. You were throwing fuel on the fire."

I swallowed, restrained myself from trying to argue with him. I spend my working life in the field of oral history and I was determined to be a good oral historian, to give my father the space to express his opinions freely. But this was one of the hardest points of the interview for me. The arguments my father made resembled so much anti-semitic propaganda. He was leaving out, or was perhaps unaware of the historical facts: Jews became moneylenders because there were few other occupations open to them at the time. And the idea that Jewish people dominated the professions and were all intellectuals is certainly a distortion. It saddened me greatly that my father carries this internalized anti-semitism.

He went on to talk about his mother.

"Often my mother says, what did I do to deserve this? By being Jewish you are exposing yourself to discrimination, to ridicule, to persecution and she says, 'I didn't choose to be Jewish.' That's one of her sayings. 'It was chosen for me by others when I was born. I could have been born Catholic or Christian and not have to go through this persecution.' I picked up this attitude from her. If somebody came up to me and said to me today, 'You're Jewish,' I would say, 'No, I'm not. I don't practice it. I don't believe in their tenets, and being associated with them has caused me nothing but grief.'"

Suddenly I remembered sitting with my grandmother the last time I visited her before she got sick. "I'm writing a book about you," I had told her proudly. She was sitting across from me on her high-backed blue velvet chair. I sat at her feet on the carpet, a third her age, in awe of her.

"And what do you write in this book about your Grananyu?" she had asked.

I blushed. "About how you have had a long life, a courageous life, a life that was often difficult because you are Jewish," I told her.

"Yes, this is true," she said, looking at me with those honest black eyes.

"And I write about finding out I was Jewish when I turned 17."

She sat up straight. "What?" she said sharply. "You have not to write about this!"

"But I want to write about it," I protested. "It is part of who I am."

"I wish you were not Jewish," she apologized. "But they count the grandmothers too so it can't be helped. I am sorry about that." I remembered our trip to Israel, how we had ascended Masada, touched the Wailing Wall, waded in the Dead Sea, how she had wanted so much to show me Jerusalem. But there she was, sitting in her velvet chair, telling me she didn't want me to be Jewish. My father inherited only her desire to hide her Jewishness, not her pride. Thus he could say to me:

"Now that you have found out, does it make any difference in your life? Yes, to some extent. There is this need for continuity, of understanding where I come from, history and genealogy. People spend tremendous amounts of time researching their ancestors. All right, so what? You are who you are now. Whether the past history influences who you are now is really up to you. It's what you let it do to you that matters.

"From an engineering point of view, my opinion is that telling you that you were of Jewish background would have had a higher cost than a benefit. Engineers analyze things in terms of cost/benefits. If we had told you that you came from this Jewish family and we immigrated, and we didn't hide the fact that we immigrated, what benefit would it have brought you? I can't quite see the big benefit there. It gives you some sense of history and some sense of background. It certainly does not open doors for you, or close doors, unless you let them be closed.

"It was not something that we sat down as a covenant and said, 'we will not tell the children.' It was understood, because we both came from backgrounds where being Jewish was extremely prejudicial for us. Now that you have learned all this, I say, so what? It's what you make of your life that counts. It's not so much where you came from."

I was stunned by my father's idea of doing a cost/ benefit analysis on the question of revealing his Jewish heritage to his children. What an absolutely rational way to approach a legacy of pain and fear. I didn't know whether to be appalled or impressed. It seemed absurd to think that the question of my linkage to hundreds of Jewish ancestors, to a whole spiritual and cultural tradition, could be submitted to the tools of engineering analysis, to a balancing column. Yet another part of me, I am after all my father's daughter, was intrigued, provoked by the question. What *are* the costs and benefits?

These are the costs: I have a profound sense of disorientation stemming from being raised with one identity and suddenly finding out we were something else. I live between two worlds: Jewish and non-Jewish, and do not feel at home in either. I was deprived of a spiritual tradition which perhaps I will never be able to connect with fully because I feel like an impostor. I did not have the guidance of my parents in learning to deal with anti-semitism; instead I abruptly discovered at age 17 that awful things had happened to my family, indeed things that were too terrifying to even talk about, a legacy of secrets and fear. Rather than having this information revealed to me slowly and explained, it was suddenly dumped on me and I had no defense mechanisms with which to process it.

Part of me wonders if my expectations are unrealistic. Even if my parents had told me that they came from a Jewish background, would they really have been capable of giving me tools to deal with anti-semitism, given their own dislocation from any positive sense of Jewishness? Could they have offered me a sense of Jewish culture, spiritual tradition, and pride?

Well, what are the possible benefits to the way I was raised? I was given an eclectic background in Catholicism, Protestantism, and Unitarianism. This gave me a wider perspective on religion than I would have had otherwise. Living in both the world of non-Jews and Jews has given me double vision—an ability to see into and understand a little of both worlds. And would knowing my parents were survivors of Nazism have prevented me from growing up with so much fear? Maybe I would have been even more afraid as a child.

The relative costs and benefits of my parents' decision to raise me completely assimilated are beside the point. What makes me angry is that my father and mother did a cost/benefit analysis on my future identity, and made a decision for me. Perhaps all parents make these decisions, want to shield their children from harm. But if Jewishness is a choice, why wasn't it a choice for me? Did they assume I would find out one day, when I was older, all on my own? They made a choice for me. I can't help but see this as a form of control, as benign and loving as their intentions certainly were.

Perhaps my parents gave me the only protection they knew how to give: the protection of passing, of camouflage, of silence and secrets. Cloaked in red curls, in Catholicism and California landscapes, baptized, shed of the old world of pogroms and quotas, they wished me safe. They wanted for me a brave new world of open freeways and endless beaches, of sunshine and public libraries. If the price of this freedom was spiritual confusion, loss of heritage, rootlessness—what a small price to pay.

Why do I want to shed this cloak of secrets, to reclaim this ancient Jewish lineage, to struggle with the meaning of what it means to be Jewish? Am I some nostalgic, naive romantic? I fancy myself brave, yet my boldness has never been tested. I am no survivor of Kristallnacht, or even of blatant anti-semitic insults in a schoolyard. Is the very safety of my cloak the nurturing ground for my bravado, the bravado from which I proclaim my Jewish identity proudly, and deem to judge my parents for their decision to pass?

The desire to understand my parents' choices to shed their Jewish identity led me to history. I began to understand that their choices make perfect sense in the context of modern Western European Jewish history since the Enlightenment, which gave Jews equal citizenship, but only in exchange for full assimilation. Urban, middle-class European Jews like my parents and grandparents generally put their faith in this assimilationist covenant, which promised acceptance in exchange for surrendering their religion and customs, gaining a Western education, and adopting the dominant culture.

Like many Jewish men of that generation, both my Hungarian Jewish grandfather and my German Jewish grandfather served in World War I. My aunt has told me that my grandfather, Max Bein, was even called down to Nazi headquarters and given an award for his service in administering a hospital during World War I. Of course, the family was terrified because they thought he was being called to Nazi headquarters to be deported! My parents were born into highly acculturated families who considered themselves German and Hungarian, where Jewishness simply was a matter of religious traditions, not an all encompassing communal identity.

This is how my mother was able to look straight at me when I was a child and say honestly, "Being Jewish is a religion and we're not religious. Therefore we are not Jewish." After the Enlightenment, Jewishness was redefined as a question, a choice.

What is the price assimilationist Jews have paid for their freedom? "The escape from one's self as Jew became a flight from self," writes historian Barry Rubin in *Assimilation and its Discontents*. He quotes American Jewish literary critic Ludwig Lewisohn who asked, "how one could be a true and great poet if he begins by denying what is truest and greatest in himself as a man?" Life under assimilation was, as Rubin puts it, "spiritually drained." "Ghetto Jews lacked much, explained the historian Louis Namier, but "had one great advantage over us—each of them belonged in every fiber of his being to a community in which he was wholly absorbed, in which he felt himself to be a fully privileged member." Both as a lesbian and a feminist I am wary of romanticizing

Jewish life in the ghetto. My life has certainly benefited from individualism and modernity. Yet I, child of assimilated Western European Jewish intellectuals, search for spiritual meaning. I search for a life beyond Zwig's bitter salt, dust, and wandering, like my father, I search for myself, for home.

I got up to make more tea. It was very late, but I was afraid if we went to sleep there would be no more opportunity to continue this conversation. My father took off his glasses and rubbed at his nose where the glasses had left a red mark on his olive skin. We shifted away from the more philosophical thoughts about Jewish identity and returned to the details of his life as an immigrant wandering from country to country.

"When you said you wanted to interview me and sent me your questions I said, Gee. All she is going to focus on is my immigrant status and this is something I've been trying to de-emphasize all my life. There was a certain amount of discomfort. A feeling of, well, there's more to me than just being an immigrant. Here in the States, I've tried to adapt. When somebody points out, 'Oh you have a slight accent,' I have this feeling of—well, my mask has been removed? Then I laugh and I say, 'Well yes, my background is from Hungary. I was born in Hungary. But I've been here many, many years.'

"Right now my home is in the States and probably will be for the rest of my life. Home is where I hang my hat. *Földönfuto.* I knew you were going to ask me about that word again. *Föld* is earth. *Futni* is running. *Földönfuto* is someone who is running across the earth, someone who makes their home by moving from place to place."

Földönfuto. One who runs upon the earth. I sat there, captivated by this image of wandering. It became hard for me to concentrate on what my father was saying. Do my father's wanderings explain why I am mesmerized by the paths of migration in the natural world? Aphids and spiders drift up in the sky, caught in thermal updrafts, frozen, lifted high into the air on invisible gossamer threads, then dropped hundreds of miles away, where they thaw and begin to gnaw on someone's roses.

They say no matter where you travel, even in the Negev or the Mojave, the pollen follows you, carried on the wind. Particles of dust from the Sahara travel a continent away. Rufous Hummingbirds migrate from their winter sites in Southern Mexico to their spring nesting places in Alaska. The whole journey is accomplished flying from blossom to blossom.

Animals migrate—birds, whales, seals, butterflies. How do they find home? No one really knows how they do it. The moon, the stars, the sound of wind moaning against distant mountains, of surf sliding against some far shore, detected at levels beyond the human ear's capacity? One scientist performed surgery on pigeons and discovered a tiny chunk of magnetite in their brains. He says that through this magnetite pigeons can sense the magnetic field of the earth, and he claims that humans have this chunk of magnetite as well. He drove a bus full of blindfolded people out in the country, let them out in a field, turned them around a few times, took off the blindfold and asked, "Which way is home?" Most people pointed in the right direction.

Where is the magnetic chip in my brain, the chip that will tell me how to find it: home. Maybe I don't have one. Maybe they moved too much, my family. Maybe the chips adapted so many times they are no longer calibrated correctly. Maybe somewhere between Germany and Turkey, Russia and Venezuela, Los Angeles and Budapest, the chip broke. And we will live forever in exile.

"Irene," my father's voice broke into my reverie. "Are you getting too tired? Should we continue this another time?"

"Oh no," I sat up straight, bringing myself back to this living room, to the hum of the freeway below us, to the taste of evening smog in my throat. "I want to keep going." I looked at him. "How did you and your parents cope with all this wandering?"

"My father's philosophy, and by extension my philosophy, was that as we moved from country to country, we adapted to the place we had moved to, as much as possible, within limits. We tried to blend in rather than stand out. Because, as the Japanese say, 'the nail that sticks out gets hammered.' "We tried to blend in, to become a part of the culture. But my father always said, 'up to a point.' And at that point you maintain your identity and your personality. You don't adapt to everything. There was always a limit and there was no confusion about where the limit was. For example, they sent me to Catholic school. I was a little boy, so I was very much influenced by the Catholic religion. The Brothers believed things that my parents did not approve of, like, for example, that God is contained in the wafer. My parents would say, 'That's very unlikely. It's a symbol.' They would try to clarify for me where the Catholic religion crossed the line in beliefs that they could not accept. The Catholics say we are all sinners. That creates a huge amount of guilt in people. My mother had to have talks with me, saying, that's a little going too far. We really don't have this sin. We are good people. Sometimes we are sinners and sometimes we are not. But the Catholic religion says you are a sinner unless you prove otherwise."

I feel endlessly adaptable and I wonder how much of this ability I inherited from my wandering father. My speech is permeated by the accents and idiomatic expressions of everyone I have ever loved: Minnesota, New Jersey, Boston, Wisconsin, Hungary, and Los Angeles are peppered together. Valerie Jean and I were constantly mistaken for each other on the phone, and once, hearing my own voice on our answering machine, I mistook it for hers.

This adaptability of speech is mirrored in my flexibility. I have traveled with women who like to drive ten hours straight; I have taken trips with those who like to meander and stop along the way. I can live with almost anyone—adapting my level of messiness to that of my housemates. My eating habits span the range from vegan to hamburger-relishing carnivore, depending on my company.

At age 35 I began living alone for the first time, and it has only been in these last few years that I have begun to discover what my true habits are if left to my own devices. I am trying to determine that point beyond which I should not adapt, the point my grandmother and grandfather spoke of to my father when he was a little boy. Discovering these boundaries is not easy for me. I am a child of assimilation, with a highly developed sensitivity to others' moods and desires, and not much knowledge of my own. I am an expert at fitting in, at making other people feel comfortable. I am the consummate immigrant. I am a "citizen of the world."

I sat looking at my father with new eyes. Hearing the whole story of his life at once suddenly threw him into relief and he seemed a stranger, not the father I had known at all. Was my father ever really a skinny Hungarian boy with a blond crewcut, in leather suspenders? Was my father a Russian schoolchild in a fur hat, a Turkish teenager hiking by the Sea of Marmara? Was my father a Catholic boy taking confession in a French Catholic school, a Venezuelan cash register mechanic? I know my father as an American engineer. My father had a station wagon and a German Shepherd and a wife with blue eyes and brown curly hair. My father went on camping trips with his two children, who were two years apart. My father got a divorce. My father remarried, an American woman from rural Iowa. My father takes trips to Europe, to England and Norway, and a ship through the Panama Canal. My father worked for the same engineering company for 34 years. My father wanders the Internet, a citizen of cyberspace, a country without borders.

I took a deep breath and asked if he remembered experiencing anti-semitism as a child.

"Let me tell you a story," he began. "One day when I was a little boy I was out playing in the park by myself. I had a little toy sailboat. There was a shallow pool, safe for children in the park. I was sailing my boat. I would launch it and the wind would pick up the sails and take it across. Then I would run around the pool and pick it up on the other end, and I'd have a wonderful time. All of a sudden these four or five, much older boys came up. I was about seven and they must have been in their teens. They started calling me a Jew boy. For some reason they knew. I don't know how. I don't know how they knew that. Maybe they asked me and I was innocent enough to say yes. They took my sailboat away. I started crying. I was very upset. They took off. There were gangs like that roaming in Hungary in 1937. There was quite a bit of anti-semitism.

"I was sitting there crying. Of course I couldn't do anything about it. I was much younger. I was one guy against four or five. I wasn't about to pick a fight with all those guys. Then, out of nowhere out come another half a dozen or so guys, about the same age as the ones that persecuted me. They asked me, 'What happened, why are you crying?' I told them the Jew boy part. They said, 'Oh, we'll take care of it.' They were Jewish guys. They were in a gang too and they made it their mission to protect against this kind of thing. They took off and disappeared behind a corner. Ten or fifteen minutes later back they came, with my boat. They said, 'We took care of it. Now leave. Don't stay here.' That's the earliest impression I have of being singled out because of my religion."

Then he talked about his conversion.

"When I was nine my mother and I converted to Catholicism. I knew some of what was going on, but I didn't know the full details. I could see that my mother was very nervous and very upset about having to do this. My father was no longer there. He was already in Turkey. He went a year or so ahead of us to get a job and get settled, and my mother stayed in Hungary with me. She was a doctor at a hospital. My father could see that this situation was only going to get worse, so he made all the arrangements. And one of the arrangements was that we had to . . . in Hungarian the expression is turn-out, in other words become Christian, in order to be able to leave. Because already the situation was bad enough that if you were Jewish you would have trouble leaving. This was very hard for my mother. I think she hid it from her parents because they would have been terribly upset. She never told them what she was doing. I was aware to some extent of what was going on, but of course at the level of a nine-year-old. I didn't understand the details, but I was brought up to accept that if my mother says so, that's the way it is."

I tried to imagine my father and my grandmother undergoing this forced conversion in those years of terror. I thought of all my father had adapted to. How had he managed to survive all this change in his life? I looked at him sitting on the couch and glanced at the tape recorder between us. There was a little bit of tape left. "Ernie, what's your philosophy of life?" I asked.

He smiled at me. "My first thought is Shakespeare— 'to thine own self be true'—because I think that's at the bottom of everything. If you try to be something that you're not, you are living a lie. When you're living a lie, sooner or later it will come out. Even if it doesn't come out, there will be this constant tension inside you between who you really are, and who you are trying to be."

I was struck by my father's reflections on this tension that haunts someone who is trying to be what they are not.

Does he feel this kind of tension inside himself? Is the fiction my parents have created about not being Jewish part of the cause of the anxiety that pervades their personalities? Or have they so completely assimilated this lie that they no longer even feel the contradictions deep inside themselves? I didn't dare ask my father this question.

I sat in my father's living room in Los Angeles remembering the time, a few years earlier, when we had searched for the brick house we lived in before the divorce. We drove down the boulevard past the zoo and the fountain, the park where the little open train still chugged round and round going nowhere. But we made a wrong turn, and had to circle again.

We had both laughed nervously. "After all those years we lived here I can't believe I made a wrong turn," my father said. Finally we found Amesbury Avenue and drove up to the brick house we both remembered. "Now it would be worth half a million and we bought it for $40,000," my father moaned, and I said, "But in this earthquake country it could be a pile of bricks," to make him feel better.

I was quiet in the car. I saw that glass again, the one my father threw at my mother just before the divorce, when my mother declared she was going back to work. I watch it shatter on the yellow kitchen wall over her head. The glass is amber, with square textured sides, a small juice glass. Was it full of juice? I don't remember any liquid spilling down the walls, only the silence at the table afterwards.

My father and I had sat in the car, engine idling. I looked down the brick walkway lined with ivy leading to the heavy wooden door. My teenage self, in stretch pants and a baggy yellow T-shirt saunters out to sweep the pine needles off the front sidewalk. My father is brooding on the floor with the lights out. I step by his dark head and his tears, ignore him, go out to sweep the sidewalk.

I looked at my father sitting next to me in his living room. I sat up and leaned over to hug him goodnight. He looked up, startled. "Good night, Irene. Sleep well," he said, reaching out cautiously to stroke my head.

VI.

REVERBERATIONS OF SILENCE: MY MOTHER'S STORY

My mother as a child in Nuremberg, Germany

MY MOTHER'S CALIFORNIA

"Children lived in constant fear. In contrast to cases of severe one-time trauma, most children living under the Nazi yoke experienced multiple traumas. There were acute assaults and chronic stress, along with sudden, repeated abandonments and uprooting."
—Judith Kestenberg

The train to my mother's house travels through the Santa Clara Valley, past remnants of apple orchards, winds through the Salinas Valley and its vast lettuce fields, skirts miles of newly planted grape vines. I like to feel the belly of the train slide across the golden grass, to see the thickets of blackberries, poppies and fireweed blazing along the tracks, the secret canopies of oak trees.

The train skims over the rich brine of Elkhorn Slough. Great Blue Herons rise from the pickleweed, screech at our wheels. Escaping the freeway, I ride through Brussels sprout fields, then south along the Santa Lucias, where the underground Salinas River emerges out of cracked earth.

The Coast Starlight sways very slowly on wild grassy land by the sea, land no one sees unless they take this train, or they test bombs on Vandenberg Air Force Base, fire missiles across the ocean towards Japan. I rode the rails south. I wanted to ride forever that day, through the Mojave and the Colorado Deserts, past the palms fringing the Salton Sea, across the patrolled border into Mexico, Central America, past Venezuela, where my father walked the streets looking for work. I wished I could continue to the tip of South America, to Patagonia where elephant seals challenge each other to bloody duels. Like my father, perhaps, I wanted to ride the rails forever, rootless and memory-free.

But I instead I was going where I had journeyed so many times, to Ojai, to my mother's redwood-shingled ranch house, to a valley where bears once feasted on cow carcasses under the Topatopa Mountains, where condors soared dark in arid skies. I was going to a place where condominiums now seem to belong, to a part of California where my Jewish family now seems to belong, my uprooted people, Jews, whom my grandmother called "citizens of the world."

This is my mother's California: the California dream the way it's supposed to be—the Ojai Valley, its orchards of oranges, vibrant green foliage laden with juicy globes—the California of the orange crate label. The sun itself was incarnate in this bold fruit suspended against the layered tilt of Topatopa Mountain behind the town. Ojai, insulated from the suburbanization of the 1990s, or at least it seemed that way. Ojai, the California that Hollywood courted and created—her sleepy streets, red-roofed adobes, her ancient oak trees. The oak trees in Libby Park captured the glow of the sunset in their rough limbs. The light tugged gently on my legs, too, and the oak trees, the land itself, called me, drew me toward the Sespe Sanctuary, the last refuge of the California condor. southern California seduced me with its lure of orange blossoms and warm seas, palm trees, evening breezes which wafted down from the foothills, carrying the faint aroma of burning chaparral.

That night my mother asked, "Would you like to see the poem I wrote yesterday?"

It's one of the things I treasure about my relationship with my mother—that we share writing. My mother showed me the poem, a brave, honest poem about aging. One line troubled me, a line about a best friend left behind in Germany. The line was veiled and so vague no one else would know what she was talking about.

How could I have raised this with my mother?

Could I have said, Describe the war more. Make it real. Describe how your friend died in a camp. Describe everything you can't remember, everything you don't want to remember, everything you chose not to remember, because you would have gone crazy with fear from remembering. Yes, put it all in the poem. Everything you've never told me about your childhood and why you left and how you left.

What if my mother did remember? What if suddenly all those memories crawled out of her past, cold worms buried in an avalanche for sixty years—memory worms? What if she had sat there at the table sipping her tea, next to her plastic green and orange saltshakers, next to her Maori masks, the books by Robinson Jeffers—and she had told me about her childhood, and started crying? What would I have done, then? Would I have known how to comfort my mother, how to listen, how to hold this woman—this mother who could not teach me how to hold, or how to cry? Or would I have just sat there, a statue daughter perched politely on a white plastic kitchen chair listening numbly, a statue daughter staring out a picture window?

They were children then, I realized that night, my mother and her sister Eva, and my father too. They were children when the war happened.

She'd told me about cookies and candy. About lemon *pfeifernusse* cookies, a dunce cap full of candy they gave her her first day of school, in 1933, the year Hitler came to power. She'd told me about the Christmas tree in the town square, lit with real candles. She'd told me her German was the interrupted, half-forgotten language of an eleven-year-old. She was a child, like I was a child, only she spent her childhood in Nazi Germany.

I thought of books I'd read about that period. Was my mother yanked out of regular schools, put into a Jewish school? Did she have friends in those other schools, friends she lost? Did she watch her parents' faces, lit by terror, by the fever of years of seeking escape, of seeing the world's doors close, one by one? My mother was a child and she had no power.

One and a half million Jewish children, *Kinder*, the Jewish children of Europe, murdered. My mother, her sister Eva, and my father were among the few who escaped. Escaped and came to a new land to start a new life, to forget, to seal the memories of their childhoods in their rib cages, store them in bone marrow. "Children are adaptable," I imagine they were told. "You're too young to remember all that. You're safe now."

Who am I, I thought, sitting there looking at my mother's poem, a child raised in Hollywood, with camping trips and a blue bicycle named Charlotte, a German Shepherd named Pepper, a child of privilege and peace—who am I to call out: Remember. Remember. Tell me—what do you remember?

There is no interview with my mother in this book, because she did not want me to interview her. I told her I had interviewed my father and asked if I could talk to her. She said, "You already know all that stuff. Ask my sister. She's the one who remembers." I didn't press her. I didn't want to cause her more pain.

NUREMBERG

Between the two world wars Nuremberg became the center of the Nazi Party; the molesting of Jews in the streets became an everyday occurrence. While the annual Nazi Party rallies were in progress in the city, the Jews lived in fear of humiliation and attack.
                                                    —Encyclopedia Judaica

I am trying to imagine the city my mother was born in—this center of the Nazi Party. I am trying to imagine her as a small girl with blue eyes and wavy brown hair. There are few pictures of her. They were mostly left behind. I am trying to imagine her walking the streets of that city. I am trying to imagine her childhood. What was her walk home from school like? She has told me she can't remember being in school. She has told me her house was near the stadium where Hitler held his rallies, that she used to lie awake in the dark, paralyzed, listening to *"Sieg Heil! Sieg Heil!"* over and over again. To this day she will not attend a march or rally, even for causes she believes in.

Jewish children learned to expect radical change at any time: new teachers, new classmates, and new curricula; occasionally, the

arrest of one of their fathers; and the disappearance of classmates as
families emigrated without notice. About two-thirds of Jewish
children and youth left Germany between 1933 and September
1939. (Kaplan 104)

She was eleven on that terrible night of broken glass,
November 9, 1938, the night of Kristallnacht, Crystal Night,
the awful beauty of that name, the night they broke through
the doors of her parents' two-story home, the night they
smashed the family's furniture, the night they broke the
dishes, the night she lay in that bedroom, listening, perhaps
hiding under the covers, listening to those bootsteps
climbing the stairs, closer, closer, the night she lay there in a
terror I can never imagine. Then the bootsteps miraculously
stopped. She heard her mother's voice protesting, "There's a
little girl in there." Somehow my grandmother found the
courage to stop those Nazi men from entering Clara's room.
If they had entered that room, how would my mother's life
have been different? I wonder what happened after the men
finally left the house. Did her mother come in and gather her
close? Or did she leave her up there alone and hide in her
own bed?

Assailants, wielding hatchets and axes, ravaged Jewish homes and
businesses, while others used incendiary bombs and dynamite to
demolish synagogues. Mobs destroyed holy items and books and
plundered Jewish homes while forcing Jews to watch. Rowdies
rounded up Jews—women and men—half dressed or in their
pajamas and herded them into the marketplace or main squares to

taunt them. Firemen and police looked on or prevented aid as synagogues and other Jewish property burned, attempting only to save neighboring "Aryan" buildings from destruction. (Kaplan 122)

There is an encyclopedia that tells me in 1939 only 2,611 Jews remained in Nuremberg. But this was my mother's family. This was my mother Clara, her sister Eva, her father Max, her mother Erna, and my great-grandmother Marie. They were five of those Jews.

Between 1934 and 1939, thousands of parents made the agonizing decision to send their children out of Germany and into the unknown, either on what were called "children's transports" or by themselves. . . . For parents, the decision to send off a child was the most excruciating moment of their lives. (Kaplan 116)

In spring 1939, Max and Erna put my mother and her sister on a train to England, as part of the Kindertransport program that rescued German Jewish children and brought them to England to be adopted by British families. I asked my mother once how she felt when her parents put her on that train. She was almost twelve years old when that happened, but she said she did not remember how it felt to be separated from her parents in the middle of a war, as Jews were being beaten and deported from the streets. She sat in her orange easy chair in California and shrugged her shoulders when I asked what she remembered. "Not much," she said. "I don't remember much."

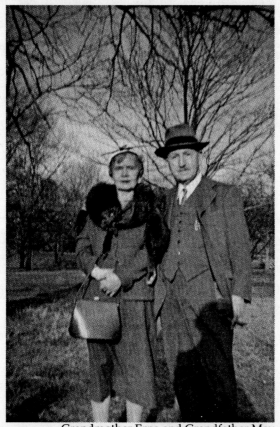

Grandmother Erna and Grandfather Max

Max and Erna were trapped in Nuremberg after their daughters left, trying to get papers to emigrate to the United States. One of Max's relatives had emigrated to Florida years earlier, and had provided an affidavit vouching that he would support the family. But the quotas for emigration were tiny. As year after year passed, they grew ever more desperate. By August 1939, almost all the paperwork was completed. Max and Erna sold the house at a huge loss, packed a moving van, and prepared to leave. Then the war broke out. Realizing it was now or never, my grandparents left the moving van in the driveway. They took a train to the border with Holland and illegally walked across, undoubtedly with hundreds of other refugees doing the same, last- ditch thing. It was thus that Max and Erna came to America with nothing, sent for their daughters in England, and began their lives anew as a maid and butler team.

But Marie. My great-grandmother Marie. What happened to her? My mother has a small black book she keeps in a drawer in her kitchen. She has always had this book with broken binding and yellowing tattered pages inscribed with delicate German script. This was Max's, the genealogy book which he filled with the Bein family tree, dating back to Alexander Bein who was born in 1775 in Frankfurt am Main, Germany. I looked for Marie's name, as my mother and I sat over cups of mint tea. She was trying to humor me, her daughter who asks questions about this painful past, who insists on knowing. I found Marie's name. "They think she died in Thereseinstadt," my mother said. "You know my parents couldn't get her out. She was too old."

Those who did not experience acute dread at least felt diffuse anxiety. One woman remembered, "The adults had been acting differently for some time. All were full of anxiety, seemed to be afraid of something that threatened their existence. And wherever two persons met, they became lost in endless discussions." Thus Jewish children grew up quickly. (Kaplan 108)

When I was a child I was told my mother's maiden name and the city of her birth: Nuremberg, a city forever to be known for the Nuremberg trials after the war, where the crimes of the Third Reich were revealed to the world. This is the city where my mother was born, my mother, gentle lover of lemon trees and poppies, of lupine-filled meadows, this is the city of her birth.

THE ATTIC OF MEMORY

"What shall I call my book?" my mother asked me that night. I leafed through the poems in her manuscript to see if I could come up with an appropriate title.

What about *The Attic of Memory?*" I suggested, taking my idea directly from a line in one of her poems.

"Well . . ." she hesitated, "I've thought of another title. How about *Reverberations of Silence?*"

"I think *The Attic of Memory* is much more powerful," I protested, but my mother had already made up her mind, and it was, after all, her book.

Our different choices for this title seem to me to symbolize the difference in how my mother and I see her life. My mother's silence about her childhood does indeed reverberate through her life, and through the lives of her children. She wants to keep it that way. I, on the other hand, think that my mother's memory lives in the attic somewhere, somehow reachable by ladder, and we should go and retrieve it; we should go clean out that attic, we could, if only she would go there, if only I could go there with her.

Perhaps there is no attic. Perhaps there only are reverberations of silence. Does my mother really not remember her childhood? Or does she choose not to talk about it because it is just too painful and this is a way to get me to stop asking her questions?

"She remembers," my aunt said, when I asked her about my mother. "She remembers, but she just doesn't want to talk about it." Maybe.

Why do I want access to the attic? And do I really? Do I want to know what is there, because I cannot imagine life without memory of childhood? Is it like walking on air or without feet, living with a great gray tide sucking at you? Do I really want to know what my mother dreams of, or why some nights she can't sleep? She lies awake, thinking. When I visit, I lie awake, holding my pee. I don't want to open the bedroom door and tiptoe down the hallway to the bathroom, because that will wake her. When I ask her too many questions about the past she can't sleep. She can't sleep, and I don't know how to comfort her. Perhaps she does remember but has told me that she doesn't so I won't have to think of her having these horrible memories. Perhaps this is yet another way of protecting me.

A PASSION FOR BOOKS

Some things I do know. My mother could not go to college when she was young. Her refugee parents had no money for such things, nor did they know about financial aid or scholarships. When she entered high school in Boston, my mother was steered to the secretarial and business track, since it was assumed she would never go to college. Her teachers knew she was bright, but did nothing to encourage her to pursue a more intellectual, academic path.

Even if there had been money, perhaps it would not have made a difference. Few girls in the 1940s were encouraged to pursue careers, and my Aunt Eva has told me that Max, their gentle but very traditional father, did not believe girls should go to university.

But my mother craved an education. In the early
1960s, home each day with two small children, she kept a
journal. She has shown me this journal, typed carefully on
her Smith-Corona manual typewriter, the pages a collage of
light and dark print, an artifact of a time of ribbons, before
word processing and laser printers. On April 29, 1964, at age
36, two days after my third birthday, she typed:

*For the last week and a half I have been reading Betty Friedan's
book,* The Feminine Mystique. *Not only have I been very much
impressed by its thesis and presentation, which are vital and well
documented respectively, but it has caused me to stop and think and
try to finalize my plans and desires for my own future. I have long
realized that having a home and children is not enough, especially
so once the children begin to grow up. Of course they may still need
guidance and help, but it is wrong to submerge one's life in their
problems.*

My mother decided to go to college. My father was
immediately supportive, suggesting that she do more than
take a few classes, but actually pursue a degree. She began at
a community college in 1964, and went on to earn her B.A. in
American Studies and her M.A. in English (Phi Beta Kappa)
in 1975 from a state university. Although she has had to take
a variety of frustrating jobs since that time, including real
estate agent and research assistant, she is now happily
teaching literature and creative writing at a local college
where she lives.

When I was a child, my mother's love of books and
knowledge electrified me. The metal bookcase near her wide

wooden desk grew heavier with books after each class she took: courses on death and dying, Shakespeare, the English novel, American literature. Most of the books were by men, but this she spoke of only later, after her feminism had grown stronger.

There were orange and yellow glossy book covers which she got for free at the college bookstore. They came flat and she folded them intricately so they would protect the precious books she carried to night class, on the evenings when our father would take care of my brother and me. Sometimes she would bring home an extra book cover and show me how to fold it over my school books. I carried those covered books proudly, showing off my "college books" to all my friends. Once in awhile she let me come with her to that legendary bookstore, where she rushed hungrily up and down the aisles, loading up her cart with Hemingway and Twain, Joyce and Dickens. Other times, I would come with her to the college library, where I did my homework in a library carrel, happily studying for hours while my mother was in class. And on long summer afternoons when the smog lay heavy on my chest, I read my mother's books: Hesse and Salinger and Doris Lessing became companions in my adolescent loneliness.

It was books she gave me, my mother. She approached them like a lover, with perhaps more trust and excitement than she felt for most people. Maybe she loved them more than people because people had hurt her in ways books never had, and books opened worlds to her far beyond her circumscribed life.

I emulated her, walking home from the public library with my arms wrapped around a stack of novels, longing for the darkened safety of my bedroom. There I would read, hour after hour, until even my mother grew worried and would urge me to go outside and play before it got dark. "You can't always read, Renie," she'd plead. "You can't always have your head in a book." I'd trudge outside to play handball with my brother or the neighbor kids, to make mud pies, or ferment rose petals into perfume with Diane, who lived next door in a house with a yard blessed with orange and lemon trees. But I always pined for the book I had abandoned.

Besides books, my mother's passion was for the long grasses of summer, shimmering in waves on the dark slopes of volcanoes, for the early mists of morning, for ducks and ducklings etching a silver line on a still pond, for water cold and clear in those days, sipped from a cup dipped directly into the lake. She taught me to shake hands with fir trees, to distinguish them from pine trees, whose needles were sharp and not at all pleasant to touch. We would lie on our backs at night and trace the paths of shooting stars as they arced across the sky. We tasted fresh raspberries and relished their juices. She taught me to hike for hours without complaining. Later, after the divorce, she taught me that a woman with two children could still go backpacking, could climb granite mountains, cross rivers, set up tents, and carry enough food on her back for a week.

My mother loved skinny dipping in Island Lake. She was free, shedding her dusty black pants, ripping open the pearled snaps of her Western shirt, returning to the green water of this small lake each summer vacation. Unfettered, she glided, her tanned arms carrying her through sunlit water. It was I who was not free, standing hot and awkward on the shore, complaining that my toes were being cut by volcanic pebbles, afraid of the needle-like dragonflies darting around my legs, afraid of sunburn and the blisters that sprouted on my singed shoulders in that era before sunscreen.

"Come on, Renie. Swim!" she'd urge, rolling onto her back luxuriously. "I can't!" I'd wail, "It's too cold." I never told my mother it was my pale plump body I was ashamed of, and how I knew I could never attain her slender brown grace, her sensuous joy. But I did long for her, and when the longing grew fierce enough I would at last force myself into the water for a few panicked strokes, thrashing the distance to her open arms, where she would hold and soothe me in a rare moment of physical closeness.

Part of the lake's magic lay in its remoteness. Three miles of rugged terrain lay between our campsite and the shores of Island Lake. There was no trail. There was manzanita bush, which scratched at skin and wove high thickets a child could get lost in. There were endless high ridges which dropped precipitously. There were stagnant pools sheltering colonies of mosquitoes. There were the ragged, rocky shoulders of a sooty mountain, which spread rubble for several miles around its base.

She knew how to find the lake. Without map or compass, with common sense and stubborn persistence, she knew. She led us over deer trails and through gullies, enticing me with sour cherry Lifesavers. It was she who had discovered the lake, alone, on a morning hike she took before breakfast, before 8:30 a.m., when she would have to return to fix my father, my brother and me pancakes and sausage. I marvel at her now, unafraid to set off at dawn across that chaotic landscape.

It was my mother's excitement which propelled me over cliffs and the mahogany legs of manzanita, over the limbs of fallen fir and pine, around house-sized rocks, in search of the lake. I remember how the adrenaline in my chest surged as she led us up that final ridge and there it would be, below us, a small green lake with an island in it, always the same, as if my mother had dreamed it. We would descend to its sheltered shores. And then my mother would swim.

THE DOUBLE WALL

She calls me every two weeks. We speak for over an hour—about our writing, favorite books, my feminist publishing, the classes she's teaching. My friends are envious. "You're so lucky to have a mother who really understands you, who is a feminist, a writer!"

But why do I feel it isn't okay for me to be emotional with my mother? Why do I feel I must always be composed when I am with her? I tell her almost everything that is going on in my life, but only after I think I can tell her without getting emotional. Are these limits she has placed, or have I placed them myself? Are they insurmountable? Am I protecting her, sheltering her from my sadness? Is my mother fragile? Is she tough? Is she both?

Her hugs are so quick and light I wonder if I've dreamed the brush of her thin arms across my back. My grandmother, Erna, suffocated my mother. "She was always swooping down to hug me, fussing over me. I hated it!" My mother tells me this, and I watch her back stiffen as she describes her mother's arms constricting her.

Lori's mother died fifteen years ago. She cries a little when I speak to her of this distance between my mother and me. "You still have her, Irene," she says gently, stroking my hair, "It's not too late." I want to believe this, but I don't know if it's too late to change such ingrained dynamics.

"I never wanted children," my mother has told me. "It was your father and his parents who wanted them. They insisted. But once I had you and your brother in my life I was very glad. And now you're not only my daughter but my friend," she always says.

I am a feminist, and the editor and publisher of an anthology called *Childless by Choice*. I have always admired and supported my mother for not wanting children. Perhaps I understand her desires intimately, since I have known since I was quite young that I would choose not to have children myself. Motherhood is so proscriptive for women. To be childless is always to be suspect, questionable, questioned.

But in recent years I have begun to do some of this questioning myself. I wonder about my mother's resistance to motherhood, and its effects on me. Was she afraid to have children because she would somehow have to relive her childhood as she raised a child of her own? Was she afraid to have children because she might not be able to protect us from what happened to her? "I never wanted to have children because I might have a boy and he could be drafted and I'm a pacifist," she always told me. When I was a teenager I knew nothing of the truth of her life during the war and how that life probably made her a pacifist.

"I just don't care for babies," she would proclaim. And indeed, when my nephew was born, it was I who cooed and made silly faces at him, while my mother stood awkwardly in the background, or disappeared behind a book. "I'm no doting grandmother," she would warn, and what feminist could blame her for not wanting to play that role? "When he gets older . . . when he can read it will be different," she'd promise my disappointed brother.

Is this too dangerous to write about? What did it mean to me to know from an early age that my mother never really wanted to have me? She never wanted to be a mother. She was waiting impatiently for me to grow out of messy irrational babyhood and emerge into the literary light, to become a companion in reading and feminism, a friend. This was symbolized in her asking me to call her by her first name when I was fourteen. My friends thought this was very cool. "Your mother is so hip," they said.

Now I wonder at the confusion I must have felt as an adolescent. She was my mother, but she was not my mother. She told me what to do—to put pot roast in the oven after school, to weed the garden, dust, do my homework. But she also told me disturbing stories about her life with my father, the ways he had disappointed her. We both wore our hair in ponytails tied with yarn. "We look like sisters, don't you think," she'd say. I thought our bodies should match too, though mine was always heavier and paler. So I dieted my way down to one hundred and eight pounds and then she fought with me, worried I'd become anorexic. She was suddenly my mother again.

Could she be both—mother and friend? Perhaps.

I learned to mirror my mother. Amy, my therapist, asks me to draw a picture of myself. I draw a crude stick figure with a column of scribbled red crayon, symbolizing my life force, in its belly. The column of life force does not spread its warmth throughout my body. Instead it rises in a constricted plume up through my throat and releases itself in stream of words and books I draw alongside my head.

In another therapy session I draw myself floating helplessly in a swimming pool, with a lifesaving ring around my neck. My legs dangle. I am constricted, enclosed in a plastic numbness, with mobility only from the neck up. And yes, I am perfectly safe, cannot drown. I am protected the way my parents wanted me to be, against the dangers of the world.

When did we make this pact of silence, this covenant, my mother and me? How old was I when I learned not to ask questions about my mother's childhood, about her life before her immigration to Boston? How old was I when I knew that it was not only questions that were taboo, but also emotion, that I must always avoid feelings with my mother, that it was the world of books and ideas she wanted me to enter with her, not the world of the heart. And so we built this double wall together, two heads speaking. Even as a child I must have known at some level that emotion, especially mine, was dangerous for my mother. It could serve as a magnet for her own emotion, the emotion of her traumatized childhood, the childhood she could not remember.

In writing this memoir, I am releasing my emotion in the only way my mother gave me. These words are a cry, a lament. My mother gave me words, a love of language, a belief in myself as a writer, and now I am speaking what she, even with her love of words, could not speak to the world. I am emerging from behind the double wall, no, I am tearing the wall down, no I am climbing on top of the wall and dancing on it with my whole body, and I am telling stories from my perch on the wall, I am singing on top of the wall and I am praying on top of the wall.

But this is a fantasy, no? In real life my mother tells me, half-joking, that when I publish this memoir she is going to change her name and pretend she doesn't know me. This is a child's reaction, the way my mother wants to run from my truth-telling.

My mother and I hiked up the canyon behind her house in Ojai. My mother can still hike uphill much faster than anyone in my family. She was wearing blue jeans and hiking boots that day and from behind she looked twenty five. I struggled to keep up with her, no breath left for talking. Finally, she paused on the ridge for a drink of water, drank and then offered me some. The water tasted warm and plastic. A red-tailed hawk swooped down over the meadow below the road, and flew away with something wiggling in its talons.

"Claire," I asked, "You know that train set we had when I was a kid . . ."

"Yeah?"

"That was your father's, right?"

"Yeah. It came from his toy factory."

"Well, how'd he get into the toy business?"

"His uncle took him into the family business. Oh, my father loved toys. He was a gentle man," she mused, her eyes soft. "Much older than my mother. She was the one who bossed us all around, the one with the temper. He just stayed out of the way and attended toy conventions."

"What happened to the toy factory?" I asked my mother.

She closed her lips tight, but a piece of the past escaped, like a tiny bubble. "The Nazis took it. The Nazis took the factory, and the uncle committed suicide."

Then she turned on me. "Haven't I told you all this before, Irene? Why do you have to ask me all these questions? I don't remember much. I was too little. You should ask my sister, Eva. She remembers a lot more."

I'd done it again, asked too many questions. I felt ashamed, making my mother exhume her buried childhood.

I remembered the trains. They lived in dusty yellow boxes with plastic windows and writing in German. My mother kept them in her closet, on the top shelf. Jeffrey and I grew up playing with this train set, without understanding its history. The trains roared on their black tracks through the living room on the shag carpet, past the couch with scratchy fabric, under the orange easy chair only my father was allowed to sit in. Faster and faster they circled, until they sped off the tracks entirely, sparks flying into the carpet, and my mother came running into the room where her children loomed like two giants over the tracks. "Be careful," she'd cry, "those were my father's trains."

"Where are those trains now?" I asked.

"I still have them in a special box in the garage."

Max was a gentle Jewish man who made toy trains for German children, some of whom grew up to deport Jews on trains. Did he ever think about that, after the war, or did his essential optimism, good nature preclude such macabre thoughts? I thought about my grandfather as I followed my mother up the mountain behind her house, and mused about my own love of riding trains.

My mother and I reached the summit of the mountain high above her house. The last California poppies of summer lined the road, their fiery heads lifted into the September sky. The oak trees in the canyon below were sprawling relics of California before the European Conquest. A thousand crickets sang in the heat under our feet. The whole landscape pulsed with life and death.

I opened my mouth. Another question flew out on red wings, dragon wings. "We're Jewish, Claire. Why didn't you ever tell me we were Jewish?"

I shut my mouth fast. But it was too late. My question escaped across the valley on scaly wings, blotting out the sun, soared over the ridge and cast a shadow on my mother's lined face.

She turned her whole body away from me. I watched her back tense, her thin shoulders poke out of her long silver hair. Were her shoulders shaking? I couldn't tell.

I was a dragon daughter, betraying my mother, who was a child, begging for silence in the refuge of California, the place where memory ends, sinks into the western sea, the place where immigrants remake themselves. I am the keeper of memory. But after I publish this memoir, will I be exiled?

I touched her bony shoulder. "Claire. I must be your worst nightmare."

She swiveled around and stared at my stricken face. She laughed. "My worst nightmare? Don't be ridiculous."

"Well, I'm the daughter who is writing about your secrets. You know my book is about finding out I am Jewish, about our family's history."

"Yeah. I've told you. I don't choose to identify with a religion I don't believe in . . . " she began again.

"But you know I have to write about it. You're a writer, too. You must understand?"

She nodded.

"I think part of the reason I'm on this earth is to write this story. But I want you to feel safe, Claire. How can I make you feel safe?"

"Change the names."

"That's all?"

"And don't read from the book in my home town, okay?"

"Of course I wouldn't do that."

"Irene, can I hug you?" my mother asked. "I've been thinking about how I don't hug people enough."

"Sure," I said in complete surprise. My mother wrapped her strong thin body around my soft larger one.

VII.
ONCE THERE WERE TWO SISTERS:
AUNT EVA

My aunt as a teenager in Nuremberg

"There are two attitudes which one may have about every piece of horror and injustice in the world—one is to try to forget, the other is to see that one never forgets."
—Karen Gershon

It was raining outside the dirty train windows. The January rain stretched a cape of water across the South Bay, licked the skinny legs of second-growth redwoods along the gravely tracks, entered the broken windows of old auto factories in Oakland.

I was on the train to Sacramento to see Eva, my mother's sister. My uncle Frank was waiting at the station. Frank was over six feet five inches tall and it was awkward hugging him. He grinned down at me, and said, "I haven't seen you in years, since you were wearing that poncho."

He was goading me like he always had. Frank and Eva used to call our family a bunch of hippies, though they were the ones in northern California, while we were stuck in staid Los Angeles.

Every summer, we'd stop at Frank and Eva's house. Their sons, Bill and Andy, would consent to play with my brother and me for one night. They were six and eight years older than I. Their games involved daring us to jump off bunk beds or lifting us on their shoulders like building blocks. They were tall and gawky, their hair cut into the shape of soup bowls by Frank, a career Army man who had spent his youth testing bombs. There was a third, older son, but I did not know about him then. He had run away when he was eleven, because he didn't get along with Frank, who was his stepfather. My aunt and uncle never spoke of him; he had been almost completely erased. This was yet another family secret. I met this son once as a teenager and that was the first I even heard of him. It took us another twenty years to connect, and by that time he had a son who, like his father, has now become a good friend.

Eva was waiting for me at the house. My mother had told me Eva doesn't dye her hair. She was still blonde at seventy-four, and thin, even thinner since she'd been fighting cancer. I felt like a large, sweaty lump hugging her, even though I'd worn my best black and white-checked pants, blow-dried my hair, and put on my most conservative polyester shirt. I excused myself, retreated into the bathroom with its yellow rug, yellow towels, and yellow toilet seat cover, and looked at my reflection in the mirror. My hair was frizzed into a mass, pimples standing out in the fluorescent glare. I did look like a hippie, my mother's zany daughter from Santa Cruz come to visit.

Back in the living room, Eva was waiting. She took me on a tour of the house. One whole room was filled with her paintings of birds on blue water, so realistic they looked like photographs. "I never knew you painted," I said in amazement. These birds were stunning—loons, hawks, storks, owls rendered in exquisite detail.

"Oh, it's just a few paintings," she shrugged, and turned to usher me out of the room. I stole one last look at the birds on the wall and realized they were all painted in mid-air, in flight. I wanted to soar away like them, across the Bay. I wished Eva could see Margit's paintings.

Down the hallway to the mahogany china cabinet, more European than anything my mother would allow in her house. The cabinet displayed relics: Erna's gray ostrich feather fan (how did that make it intact to America? It looked just like the one Margit had in her cabinet.), a picture of Max smiling, relaxed, by some craggy mountains.

"*Ja*, that's where he took the weight cure at the baths in Czechoslovakia every year," Eva said, smiling to herself. On the next shelf stood carved wooden men from Austria who resembled Grandfather in the movie *Heidi*, little girl dolls in blue dirndls, sailboats from Norway, bark paintings from Baja, black pots from Oaxaca. My aunt and uncle travel all over the world.

"And this is very old," Eva said, holding up what I realized was a California Indian basket, tightly woven, a black snake twisted around its golden coils. My heart sank; sweat pricked my armpits.

"Where'd you get this?" I tried to sound neutral, politely interested.

"Oh from some lady in the desert. I don't remember exactly where or when," she said, ready to move on to the next stop in the tour.

"Do you know what tribe it's from?"

"I don't know. Isn't that funny?" She stopped to peer at me for the first time, somehow aware that my question was more than casual.

I thought of Valerie Jean, her Cahuilla great-grandmother, of her lost baskets, sold off to collectors for how much, at what price? I imagined sneaking this basket out of my aunt's china cabinet. I could have put it in my backpack and taken it on the train to Valerie. She would have known what to do with it. She could have taken it to her grandmother Tutu. Tutu could have given it to her Kashaya Pomo friend Lynn, who was going to the California basketweavers' conference in Chico the next month. Or Tutu could have donated it to the Malki Indian Museum on Morongo Reservation. They would have known what tribe it belongs to, maybe even who made it.

"Come sit on the couch," Eva was saying. "Would you like tea or coffee? I have decaf too."

"Tea," I muttered, trying to recover. I sat down on the couch, crossed my legs. Eva brought me strawberry tea in a delicate white china cup with blue roses climbing down the handle into the saucer. I wondered at the difference between Eva and my mother, my mother with her gas-station-medley plate collection, and Eva with her china, and mahogany cabinets. Was it simply taste? Or was it my mother's desperate need to become American? Did she and my father select gas station plates and glasses as the farthest thing from Europe they could dine on?

Eva knew I was there for family stories. She reclined in an oak rocking chair, sipped her tea, waited for my questions. Frank retreated to his den, allowing us some time alone together.

"I was very surprised to get your letter," Eva said. "We hadn't heard from you in a long time." I had written her, asked if I could come visit and talk about family history, apologized for not being in touch for so long.

"Tell me about your father, Max." I began.

"My father? He was the gentlest man in the world. He had a soft little mustache, and loved toys. You know he ran a toy train factory," she smiled. "He traveled to toy shows all over Germany and collected samples for us. Your mother and I shared one room so we could convert the other room into a playroom, a whole room just for toys. We had every toy in the world—big dolls with real hair, wardrobes of doll clothes, kitchen sets with tiny refrigerators and stoves, stuffed animals . . ."

My eyes wandered across the living room to the entourage of teddy bears who had taken over a leather armchair. Fat brown ones with gorgeous tummies, scrawny blonde bears with large ears like rabbits, fierce, white polar bears, little black bear cubs with pug noses . . .

Eva was still talking, "*Ja*, and always there were the electric trains running through the toy room, past the kitchen stoves and the stuffed cats and dogs. Always there were the trains."

"Jeffrey and I played with one of those train sets when we were kids. My mother said you had one too."

"But I sold it," she said. "The boys grew up and then we moved. It took up too much space in the garage. So we sold it. I've always regretted it." She turned her head so her thin blond bangs covered her eyes.

Eva started talking about the war. I guess she figured that's what I was there for, to hear about the war. She pulled an old black photo album out of a drawer. "I snuck this out of Germany on the Kindertransport, when your mother and I left Germany and came to England. At sixteen, I was one of the oldest children on the transport. Your mother and I were the only two children who knew we were going to friends of the family who wanted us, would take care of us. The other kids were going to be adopted by any British families willing to take them in. Some of them didn't get treated very well. The families just wanted a maid, or extra farm labor. They didn't love the kids, didn't even notice when they needed new shoes.

"The train stopped in Cologne and several other cities, collecting children. Some of those children were so small. I felt sorry for them crying and crying for their parents. I volunteered to take care of one of them, a little six-year-old boy with red hair. He couldn't understand why his parents had sent him away. He cried all the way to England and threw up on me on the boat."

Eva was quiet. Somewhere in the house a clock chimed once. I imagined my mother and Eva, teenage girls departing on the train from Nuremberg. Were they wearing matching dirndls, carrying small suitcases? Did their parents pack them a lunch before they left? Was the station decorated in red flags with black swastikas? How many parents were there, waving as the train left? Did anyone dare cry? Or were they just numb and scared, smiling goodbye?

Eva showed me pictures of her childhood. A three-story brick house in a Nuremberg suburb. The street appeared normal, a few geraniums in a window box, an ordinary-looking sidewalk. The ornate synagogue downtown. My mother and Eva—two giggling girls playing with some stupid-looking little boy in *lederhosen*.

"Is the house still there?"

"No it was bombed. All of it was bombed, the synagogue, our house, the streets. I went back. It looked totally different. It was completely rebuilt after the war."

Eva turned the page. "These are the official pictures."

Did she mean passport pictures? I was afraid to ask. There was my mother in a dark dress with a Peter Pan collar, her wavy brown hair yanked tightly to the side into a barrette, her hazel eyes staring off. I had never seen my mother look like that. She looked like she was in a trance, drugged. Those were not my mother's eyes.

There was Eva, her blonde hair much shorter than now, pulled tightly also to one side, her blue eyes staring off, but not drugged. No, I realized, Eva was not numb. Her eyes were full of pain. Her girl mouth was slightly open, hurt. My mother's spirit was gone in the picture, but Eva's was not. Eva was all there, watching everything.

"Why did they do that to your hair?"

"So they could see one ear."

I didn't ask why they needed to see one ear. From somewhere I recalled a book on Nazi eugenics, a manual on how to recognize a Jew, drawings of Jewish noses lined up on the page.

There was a picture of Erna.

On her photo a child had scrawled in black ink, "Mama." I wondered if Eva had taken this picture out to look at in England, maybe after everyone had gone to bed. Did she cry, "Mama," and think of her parents stuck in Germany? In the picture Erna was fierce, lips drawn tight, shiny brown hair bouncing the light back hard out of the picture, eyes narrow and furious.

No. I looked closer. Erna's eyes were sad and shiny; her lips thin with the weight of holding in anguish. Which was it? Who was the real Erna—the bossy, harsh woman my mother and Eva remembered, or this sad woman with pain in her face? Were they both real?

There was Max, "Papa" scrawled under his picture. He wore a stiff collar and elegant tie, gray suit. Max had hardly any hair left on his head—they didn't have to worry about his ears showing— and his long, handsome nose dipped toward his small mouth. Looking at that picture, I realized Max gave me his shy mouth. Max looked like a startled coyote, brown eyes wary, ears standing out big and alert by his face, chin pointing forward.

There was Marie, the grandmother they left behind. Eva explained, "Only four visas came through. Four. One for your mother. One for me. One for my mother. One for my

father. Marie was too old to qualify. We had to leave her in
her apartment in Augsburg."

Eva's blue eyes contemplated me across the dark
living room. Rain dripped off the gutters. I resisted an urge to
pick up one of Eva's fat teddy bears and cuddle it. It was an
ordinary day in Sacramento. How could we be talking about
such things?

I took a deep breath and looked at the picture of Marie
again. Hair piled up, full figure imposing in a long dark
dress, she was elegant. Eyes, they were almost Asiatic, and
bright with laugh lines at the corners. I realized my mother
has Marie's eyes. So does Eva. They are my eyes too. Marie
gave all of us her eyes.

Eva put the album away. I ventured, "Could I have
copies of those pictures sometime?"

She rocked her chair hard, swallowed. "Well," she
hesitated, "They're very fragile. I'll look into it. Do you have
more questions?"

"Well, a few. Is that okay?"

"Just a few more. You know this is difficult to talk
about, Irene." She looped a pale finger tightly through her tea
cup.

"I know. Just one more question."

"*Ja* . . ."

"I've read about Kristallnacht . . ."

"*Ja.*"

"Where were you then? What happened to you?"

For a moment, I wasn't sure Eva was going to answer.
I studied the lines around her eyes, her pale face. Finally my
aunt said, "Kristallnacht. Night of Crystal. Those words

make it sound so beautiful. But God what a terrible night that was.

"I wasn't there. I was in Frankfurt, in housekeeping school. Our family needed money. I was old enough to work, so my parents sent me to learn to be a maid. My mother told me what happened later. The Nazis burst through my parents' front door and threw their furniture and china against the wall. My father wasn't home, I don't know where he was. They searched the entire house, except for Clara's room.

Eva paused. "I've always felt terrible that I wasn't there that night. And you know the amazing thing was that they didn't arrest my father and imprison him."

"How come they didn't arrest Max?"

"They tried. They came to the toy factory, two Nazis, to arrest him. It was the morning after the pogrom. The city was destroyed, the streets littered with glass from shattered windows and rubble from burnt buildings. The Jewish schools were closed. Hardly any Jews went out of their houses. It was the same way in Frankfurt. I'll never forget the silence of that morning after the night filled with screaming and breaking glass—"

Eva faltered. I wondered if I should ask her to keep speaking.

But she picked up the thread. "My father, he always went to work. He rarely missed a day, even with a fever he would put on his suit and go off to the toy factory with his little lunch wrapped in wax paper. He saved that wax paper and re-used it day after day. So that day, despite my mother's protests, he went to work. Most of his employees were not

Jewish, so the factory stayed open. That morning they came, two Nazis.

"'Herr Bein,' they summoned my father.

"My father was a mild man and I think he would have gone with them without protest. But the employees did something incredible. They came, from all corners of the factory, pouring off the assembly line and the secretarial offices and the marketing department. Somehow, the word got around instantly of what was about to happen. They surrounded Max, over a hundred of them. They said to the Nazis, 'You can't take Herr Bein. We won't allow you. Not Max Bein.' And a miracle happened. Those two Nazis left."

"They resisted the Nazis, these employees, for your father? They must have really liked him even though he was their boss."

"Everyone loved Max. Still, it was a miracle. So many friends of mine lost their fathers that night."

It was time for lunch. Frank joined us at the small table in the kitchen under a cuckoo clock. I remembered another cuckoo clock which hung on my bedroom wall when I was little and threw huge menacing shadows across lonely walls.

Roasted turkey sandwiches on gold-rimmed china. Uncle Frank regaled me with stories of San Francisco in the good old days when he was a child, when the Fillmore was Jewish and he played on the sand dunes that covered what are now the Sunset and Richmond districts. Frank dashed up and down the hills of the city, up and down, before all the houses were built after the war. There was no Golden Gate

Bridge then, only the fog pouring through the open mouth of the bay.

Then Eva laughed, told the story of how she met Frank at the Jewish center. She was sitting there, and this man behind her was pontificating. She thought, that is the most opinionated man I've ever heard. Then he asked her out and she ended up marrying him.

Lunch was over. We were back in the living room. Frank was in his study reading. Rain blurred the view out the window toward the Sierras, fell on the covered swimming pool.

"What was it like when your family came to the United States?" I asked my aunt.

"My parents worked as a maid and butler team. I sewed belts in a factory. Twelve dollars a week. I gave ten dollars to my parents, used one dollar for carfare, kept one dollar for myself. I saved those dollars. As soon as I could, I bought my first American dress. My clothes looked too German. You understand?"

I nodded.

"No boys would date me. Then I had to register as an enemy alien, since my parents were German. Your mother did too. We needed special permission to go to Girl Scout camp at Cape Cod, since that was further than aliens were usually allowed to go."

Enemy aliens? My mother and Eva, two frightened teenagers who just wanted to be normal American girls? "I was a Bluebird," I told Eva, but she went on talking as if I wasn't there, speaking to a blank spot on the opposite wall.

"I sewed belts while your mother went to high school. *Ja*, she was the lucky one. I was so jealous of my sister, going to school while I worked. She changed her name from Clara to Claire. She doesn't even have an accent. My mother said Claire was the smart one. I was the pretty one. I had already finished high school in Germany and my parents believed women didn't need to go to college. Besides, we didn't have any money. In Germany, I had gone to a Jewish high school. They still have reunions every year and I always go. The most recent one was two years ago. Frank came with me. But I think this might be the last reunion. Everyone is getting old and dying now." Eva sighed.

"So Max became a butler?"

"*Ja*. I remember when his employer wanted him to learn to drive so he could be a chauffeur too. My father took the car out and drove it into a hole. That was it. He swore he'd never drive again. He never did. Neither did my mother."

I took a big breath, "Eva? Do you know my parents never told me they were Jewish?" I thought Eva knew, but I wasn't sure.

"Oh yes," she said. "We weren't supposed to say anything. It was hard when you came to visit every summer. We had to coach the boys."

"But, you consider yourself Jewish, don't you?"

"*Ja*, but I'm not religious. We only go to Temple for the High Holidays. I do volunteer at the Temple gift shop once a month, and the boys were bar mitzvahed."

"Well, what do you think of the choice my mother made?" Instantly, I knew I probably shouldn't have asked that question, it put Eva in a hard spot, but I just had to ask it.

Eva shifted her thin legs. "Your mother and I are very different. I was four years older when the war happened. I remember a lot more."

"Yeah, you do remember a lot more. I don't know why she forgot everything. Maybe it's the age difference, maybe personality. I guess people just deal with things differently."

She leaned forward. "I hope you aren't asking her these kinds of questions, Irene."

"Oh no." I took one last sip of strawberry tea. "Well, what do you think being Jewish is? Is it a religion, like my mother says? You're not religious, but you still call yourself Jewish."

"I think Jews are a people, with a history, a culture," she answered quietly, but with certainty.

"Yes. That's what Margit, my grandmother, says too."

Eva smiled. "I like Margit. I miss seeing her since the divorce."

Eva and I went out to the kitchen. She put pots and pans away. In between the clatter I asked, "Don't you think my mother has forgotten her childhood because of the trauma she experienced in Nuremberg, the way women who were abused as children often don't remember what happened to them?"

Eva straightened up to stare at me. "But nothing bad happened to us in Nuremberg." she said. "Now it *was* hard in England when the man we were living with said if your mother didn't learn English more quickly he would send her back to Germany . . ."

I was dumbfounded. My aunt had just finished telling me about Kristallnacht. Did Eva have her own blocking mechanisms? Did she compare their experiences to the experiences of people in the camps, and then minimize them? Or did she truly believe nothing bad happened?

I felt odd around my aunt, almost shy. I could read her body language so easily because it's a lot like my mother's. They share a sadness, fragility, a sweetness, a kind of innocence. She is still pretty, too. I know I don't really know my aunt, but she is no stranger. I actually look more like her than my mother. I have her fair coloring and now that I am older my hair is more blonde than red. When I looked at this woman whom we visited a few times a year when I was a child, whom I hadn't seen much of as an adult, I felt wistful.

It was time to go. I hugged Eva goodbye on the stairs to the garage. There wasn't much of her to hug. Eva held me for a second and her bones poked at me a little. I hope the chemo will work, I thought. Eva hugged me gingerly. I wondered if she hugged me this way because I was sweaty, because I asked too many questions and upset her, because she didn't feel well, or because I was Claire's daughter—the dyke. Was Eva afraid to get too close because I didn't visit much? Maybe I just came to get my questions answered and then I would disappear. Or maybe Eva hugs everyone that way.

VIII.

KEEPER OF MEMORY

Irene and Lori Dancing at the 1998 Jewish Renewal Kallah

ZAKHOR: TO REMEMBER

"Zakhor, the biblical commandment to remember, has been a
fundamental responsibility of the Jewish people throughout history.
From remembering one's ancestors to recalling one's enemies,
there is a flow to the year that rests on an assumption of a
consistent, continuous and common collective memory."
—Norma Baumel Joseph

To find out I was Jewish at age seventeen meant to grapple with secrets and lies in my family. But this is not that unusual a story. As I was writing this memoir, the story of Secretary of State Madeleine Albright's discovery of her Jewishness was published in *The Washington Post*. Like my parents, Albright's parents were Holocaust refugees who decided safety lay in leaving their Jewishness behind, not revealing it to their daughter. In the past fifteen years, I have met a number of people who discovered their Jewish background as adults. Some of them were adopted and learned their identity as part of locating their birth parents. Some of them were children of Holocaust survivors. Some, like my friend Jeanne, were daughters of women who had experienced anti-semitism in the United States in the 1930s and 40s, and decided to pass as a survival strategy. Jeanne and I started a support group in the late 1980s for women like us, and met other women with similar stories. We also attempted to edit an anthology of writing by women who found out they were Jewish as adults. We received powerful letters from women all over the country with this experience, but hardly anyone, including us, was able to write about it.

When the secrets are familial in nature, when the taboo against speaking runs so deep, to write our stories is sometimes tremendously challenging.

There is a startling tradition of secret Jewish identity across the globe. Throughout Latin America and the U.S. Southwest there are Jews who converted because they were persecuted by the Inquisition in Spain back in the 15th century, but kept practicing Judaism secretly. In recent years, people in the former Soviet Union and in Eastern Europe have uncovered their Jewish identity. In Brazil, it is estimated that out of a population of 150 million people, there are fifteen million *conversos*, only three million of whom know the truth about their Jewish descent. The Pathans of Afghanistan and Pakistan are Muslims who fought to drive the Soviets from Afghanistan a few years ago, and believe they are the descendants of the northern kingdom of Israel, exiled to the mountains of Afghanistan by King Sennecharib of Assyria in 722 B.C.E. In Eastern India live the Sinlung, a Mongoloid tribe who originally lived in the Chinese Tibetan borderlands. Hundreds of years ago they fled Chinese persecution, and found refuge in Eastern India. They hold sacred a mythic ancestor named Menasi, and believe they are descended from the Israelite tribe of Manasseh, one of the sons of Joseph. In Zimbabwe, the Lemba, a tribe of 100,000 Blacks, claim descent from the Israelites who came there to work in mines and on seafaring vessels in the time of King Solomon and Maqueda, Queen of Sheba.

My family is part of a long tradition, an ancient legacy of dissolution and dispersal. What a legacy. So many centuries of hiding, in so many lands. After only one generation of silence and secrecy, I'm confused enough. I wonder, why is it so important to maintain Jewish identity in secret for so many years as the *conversos* have done? What is it about being Jewish that survives in some vestige of an identity—candles on Friday night, a fringed shawl buried in a drawer, a silver star on a thin chain—what is it about Jewishness that persists, despite all the odds?

This Passover, I, for the first time, performed the ritual duty of breaking the middle matzoh, which represents what has broken off from the Jewish people. I was amazed when we went to search for the matzoh that I was the one who found it.

So much writing today, both fiction and nonfiction, speaks of two things: memory and place—a yearning for roots, and a yearning for home. This memoir is no different. I write of a family, a culture in exile, displaced, rootless. I write of a family which in some senses has lost its memory, chosen assimilation, amnesia. These are not unique themes; they are absolutely modern and absolutely American.

I still live in Santa Cruz, the place I came to attend college, and found refuge from Los Angeles. Tall redwood trees encircle the library where I work each day. The trees seem ancient, but these mountains were ruthlessly clearcut less than a hundred years ago. It is left to me to imagine the original endless forests, to reconstruct my family's Jewish past from a few family stories, from books I check out in this library.

In 1989 I began working at the oral history office at UC Santa Cruz's University Library. While it was my background in publishing which qualified me for this position, it is remarkable and perhaps destined that I have ended up in a profession dedicated to the recovery of memory and history.

My parents too, in their own way, seek to remember. My mother's kitchen cupboards are stacked with photo albums, high school yearbooks, scrapbooks of trips she has taken, a diary of her life at the oil refinery town in Venezuela where my parents lived when they were first married, a diary recording my first three years of life, fifteen years of her own poetry carefully filed in notebooks. My mother recently surprised and touched me when she opened a file drawer that contained my childhood artwork—pictures rendered in yarn, fingerpaint and gold-sprayed macaroni.

My father has documented almost every telephone conversation I have had with him on small scraps of paper. "Making $3.50 an hour, not happy. Likes college roommate, taking environmental studies classes." He has archived these scraps in a folder, along with the letters I write.

It was my father who created four videotapes preserving our family's life: 1962-1974, assembled out of reels and reels of home movies, beautifully narrated and choreographed to music. I watch them repeatedly. Vacations to the redwoods, the Oregon Coast, the San Fernando Mission, the Santa Monica palm-lined promenade where Margit reappears six inches taller than I remember her, where she sits on a beach in a black swimsuit, her wide back mirroring my own broad shoulders, her muscles strong as she lifts her arms to wave at my mother and my baby self playing in the surf at some southern California beach. "Erna

Bein," my father announces, as my other grandmother strolls onto the promenade and takes my brother's small hand. 1965. Was she dying then? "Erna Bein." I push rewind, and watch my grandmother walk under the palm trees again. And again. And again. As if I could reverse time itself and come to love this grandmother I never really knew.

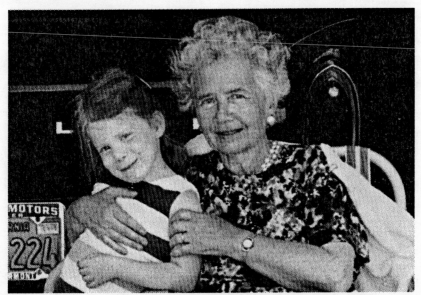

My grandmother, Erna, and me as a child, circa 1965

My father has kept a diary off and on since he was a boarding school student in Turkey some fifty five years ago. Both my parents carry video cameras to family gatherings. My father completed an oral history/genealogy with my grandmother before her death. Even my grandmother, who claimed to only want to look ahead, saw the importance of passing on the family's history to both my father and me. This is a family always documenting, preserving, in love with the act of remembering itself. "When I die I want you to have my journals and my poetry," my mother has told me. She knows I will care for, and seek nourishment from her words.

What is it that drives my mother and father to record their lives this way? Perhaps it was the very fragmentary nature of their early lives which planted this desire to document, some yearning for solidity and permanence? Then perhaps it is no surprise that I, too, have this desire to document, to write this memoir, to preserve the history of this family, to muse about the truth. Perhaps my words provide a missing link in this family documentary.

There is another paradox of my parents' lives—they married each other. Out of all the people in the world they could have chosen, they chose each other, two Jewish child refugees of the Holocaust. On the foundations of that cultural and intellectual affinity, they built an edifice of denial in the ripe soil of the 1950s and 1960s, where to aspire to be American and not ethnic was the greatest aspiration of all.

There is irony here. For though I was raised without memory in the gray heat of Los Angeles, I know more about my family than many of my friends know about theirs. I have family trees on both sides extending back several centuries. More than trees, lists of names, I know intimate stories about my ancestors. I know what they did, what towns they lived and died in. I have no candlesticks, but I have my great-grandmother Regina's lace doilies and ostrich feather fan. My friends were raised with knowledge of their Jewish heritage, but I am blessed with these rich stories of my ancestors.

For years I felt terrified at the very thought of "practicing" Judaism. The word practicing is so understated; it sounds like practicing basketball or piano scales. The very thought of allowing myself to feel spiritually Jewish, to celebrate and honor Rosh Hashanah, Yom Kippur, Passover, has been frightening and I am only now beginning to overcome this fear.

"I want to raise Raphi Jewish," my best friend Leslie told me. We were sitting on her bed across from each other. Her son was four months old, dimpled, searching for her breast. "I want him to know more than me. I don't feel like I know much. Like, what's the difference between Torah and Talmud?" she asked.

"But you know so much," I said in amazement. Leslie was my first Jewish woman friend. In the past fifteen years there have been many latkes and menorah lightings, many seders at her house. She is my true Jewish lesbian sister. I think of her as the one who *knows* the prayers, who knows.

"I guess I have you on a pedestal, Leslie. You were the one who taught me everything."

She laughed. "No wonder you don't feel like you know much, if I was the one who taught you! No, Renie, I want to learn more about being Jewish, about the religion and history. I've been thinking about taking a class at the Temple."

"I should do that. But I'm scared to." I paused, felt my heart begin to race.

"Why are you scared?" she asked.

"Because. . . I don't know." I swallowed, shifted my legs on her bedspread. "I can't explain it. Somehow. . . if I do that, if I were to become spiritual . . ." I looked up at my curly-haired friend, breastfeeding her son. Could she really have a son? Could we both really be approaching forty? I looked down at the bed. A chasm seemed to be opening between the pillow and the pink quilt, between Leslie and I, and I was about to fall in. I whispered. "It's about the Holocaust. If I practice Judaism then I will really be Jewish. That terrifies me. As long as it stays in my head, as long as I just read history, I'm safe. But if I start to feel spiritually Jewish . . ."

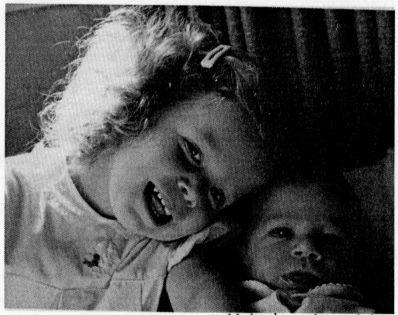

My brother and me as babies

JEFFREY

The moon illuminated charcoal mist over the sea. My brother Jeffrey and I walked along the cliffs near my house.

This was a rare and special visit for us. My nephew was at summer camp and my brother was spending a week visiting me in Santa Cruz. We talked about things we hadn't talked about in years, like our parents' divorce, and our feelings about religion.

"How did you feel when you found out we were Jewish, Jeffrey? You know, when Granapu died?"

"Surprised." It was dark and I couldn't see my brother's face, or read the emotion behind his level voice.

"Do you remember the exact moment when you figured it out?"

"Well, they handed me a yarmulke . . ."

"But how did you know what it was, Jeffrey?"

"I was old enough to know," he replied.

"So," I pursued. "What did you do with the information once you knew? Just file it away? My parents were born Jewish. I have brown hair. It's another smoggy day. So what?"

"I was an existential atheist in high school. Being Jewish was a religion and I wasn't religious. It didn't matter to me until later, I guess," my brother said. "I guess it was about ten years ago, around the time Mark was born, when I studied Hebrew and Jewish mysticism, that it started to matter."

"When I go to services, even Jewish Renewal services, I feel like an impostor," I burst out. "I feel unworthy!"

"Why, Irene?" he asked, stopping on the path to face me. His long eyelashes lit up briefly in the headlights of a passing car.

"Because I don't know enough."

"That's the way converts feel."

"But I'm not a convert! I feel this bizarre sense of being both an insider and an outsider."

"Yeah, that's exactly how I feel too," Jeffrey said. "That's what I remember about how I felt at the funeral, this weird mix of insider and outsider status. I had viewed Jews from the outside, as Other. And now *they* were me."

"Yes, I remember thinking about how I'd read *Anne Frank* as a non-Jew and cried. But how much more upset I felt thinking about that as a version of Claire's life. You know, you were fourteen when we found out. I was seventeen. Maybe that's part of the difference between us," I mused. "You lived at least part of your childhood knowing the truth. But fourteen is still pretty old." I paused, glancing at three guys partying along the cliffs, wondering how drunk they were. I lowered my voice. "Did you ever guess, when we were kids? What was your theory about our parents, why they came to the United States?"

"They were refugees."

"Well you know that now, but then . . ."

"I knew that then," he stated.

"How? How could you have known that if you didn't know they were Jewish?"

"There were other kinds of refugees from Hitler, political refugees," he pointed out.

I was fascinated by this difference in our perceptions. "Gosh, I just thought they immigrated here for economic opportunity or something. You really figured that out?"

"Sure," he said.

We continued walking. The smell of the salt stung my nose a little. The garish lights on the Boardwalk were almost magical from this distance. Delighted screams of children on the roller coaster drifted across the water. We stopped and leaned our bellies against the railing, peered down at the waves.

"I remember Claire telling us about her grandmother," Jeffrey said suddenly. "Do you remember that? She always said her grandmother had written and said she was going on a long trip and they never heard from her again."

I was stunned. Below us the sea rocked in silver waves. Out on the bay the light of a single ship met the eye of the moon. "I don't remember that at all," I almost whispered. "Really? She told us that story then?"

"Sure," Jeffrey said. "Many times. Starting when we were really little."

"Did you ever ask her more about this?"

My brother sighed. "No, of course not, Irene. I knew we weren't supposed to ask. I could hear it in her voice."

"We were raised Christian, you know," my brother proclaimed.

I exploded. "No way! No. Not Christian. Assimilated, yes. Not Christian."

"Well Irene, we celebrated Easter and Christmas. We went to Christian schools. We sang 'Hark the Herald Angels Sing' and 'Silent Night' in the choir. We wore little white robes with red paper bows at our neck, and our parents came to see us. What does that look like?"

"But that was about teaching us to fit in, to be non-Jewish. It wasn't about being Christian."

"They wanted to give us religion, the religion they never had, couldn't have," he insisted.

"No." I kicked the railing like a child. "If that was true they wouldn't have expressed this disdain, this derision for religion. You remember what Claire always said if anyone mentioned God, 'What are they? Religious or something?' I can just hear that sarcasm in her voice when she would say that. Remember?"

"Yeah," my brother admitted.

"There was no room for spirituality in that house, no respect for it. That's why I have this internalized cynicism about praying. I don't want to have it, but I do. Do you pray?"

"Yes," Jeffrey said. "I go for walks and talk with God. I have faith. It's a ridiculous thing in some ways, to cast aside rationality and have faith. But I like what it gives me. An ethical system, strength. I couldn't get that from our mother's love of nature, her pantheism. I'm both Jewish and Christian," Jeffrey said. "I am tired of trying to fit into anyone's box."

I thought of Regina and Margit and their double religion. My brother was carrying on the family tradition by converting to Methodism but continuing to define himself as both Jewish and Christian.

I was envious of my brother's ease with prayer even though I disagreed with him about pantheism's lack of an ethical system. If he could pray this easily maybe I was just messed up, should stop blaming my alienation on my parents? "But Jeffrey," I said, "Don't you think prayer is the ultimate act of rebellion? Our parents wanted to protect us from what happened to them as children."

"Right."

"So they didn't tell us they were Jewish. They constructed this whole other identity for us—Unitarian Church, Congregational and Catholic schools."

"Right." My brother was following my argument carefully, like the academic he is.

"The last thing they wanted us to be was religious Jews. If I go and practice Judaism, if I pray, that is the ultimate act of defiance. I'll blow the cover they so carefully constructed for us."

"Oh, I see," he nodded. "I don't have that problem. I haven't felt that way. But I don't understand these distinctions between being a cultural Jew and a religious Jew. The question for me is religious. To be a Jew is to practice Judaism. It's that simple. It's not a question of essence, but of practice." He turned to face me. "Do you have faith or don't you?" he interrogated me in the dark.

"I don't know." Then I laughed my head off there by the waves. I laughed because I realized I'd given the ultimate agnostic answer.

JEWISH LESBIAN DAUGHTERS OF HOLOCAUST SURVIVORS RETREAT

Last night someone said, "What matters is not so much the stories about what happened to our parents, but how this affects us today." I think this is true. Somehow this retreat, meeting all these other daughters, makes my family seem more ordinary, makes all of this less inflated, grandiose.

We've talked about relationships. Someone talked about trust, how our parents' trust in people was broken, so it is difficult for us to trust. Someone else said they felt their ability to judge character was damaged. Her parents taught her that anyone could be a Nazi; anyone could turn you in at any time. Other women here were also raised by overprotective parents, in an environment permeated with anxiety and fear. I imagine the daughters of camp survivors have experienced far more of this than I did.

We also talked about the positive things we received from our parents: a passion for life, for learning, amazing humor. It's true that survivors are some of the most passionate, zesty people I have met.

Many women spoke of it not being okay to cry in their family. Someone said she remembered falling off her bike and telling herself all the way home not to cry, because it would upset her parents. Someone said, "Everything was supposed to be okay. If I cried in front of my parents, it would worry them." Many of us spoke of numbness, or of being overwhelmed by feeling. We all seem to be working on understanding our emotional lives. Someone said, "Our parents dealt with physical survival. We are dealing with the psychological and emotional issues they couldn't afford to deal with." Detachment from feelings was sometimes essential for survivors. Those in hiding, in concentration camps, or even those who were refugees like my parents, faced extreme circumstances, where disassociation from feelings may have been the only way for them to keep thinking strategically, adapt, not fall apart. For those in hiding, crying might literally have meant death, the sound that gave them away in their hiding place.

These adaptations our parents made became the patterns which defined our emotional lives as children, and now as adults. As one woman said, "There was no space for us to have feelings. We took care of our parents." Someone else spoke of her father's fits of rage, the only way he expressed his feelings. I thought of Granapu's rage.

This morning I am finding solace high on the ridge alone here writing, watching a family of quail disappear into the elfin forest. It's hot. Vultures swing down the valley. Below I can hear the talking and laughing of the daughters.

We sat in the lodge last night. Someone played a mandolin. On the dark walls above our heads hung several large velvet, painted tapestries. One depicted four deer in a clearing in early spring, ice just melting off the river. Another, over the door to the kitchen, was of a huge golden stag thrusting his swollen chest out over a valley in fall.

My mother has these same tapestries in her house, smaller versions. She got them years ago, at the Black Forest Inn in a small town in northern California. We used to go there once a year on our way to summer vacation. It's a German place, the Black Forest Inn. My mother will not call herself a Jew or a survivor, but when I was young she did tell me that she was born in Germany. When I was a child, this was my heritage—this restaurant we visited once a year, where we ordered goulash or Wienersnitzel, where my parents spoke German with the owner, and once, long ago, before the divorce, they danced together under these same velvet tapestries.

One year, perhaps when I was eleven, my parents bought two of those tapestries and took them home, along with a family of plastic deer, a daddy, a mommy, and two fawns, that still stand on the mantelpiece of my mother's living room.

I have known I am Jewish for over half my life and yet part of me is still that shy, small child, playing with her goulash, wishing she had ordered a hamburger. Last night, I sat with this tribe of daughters in a lodge in northern California under those same tapestries, tapestries I have seen nowhere else. I wondered at this thread connecting my past and present.

I love being with this group of daughters of survivors, all lesbians. That we are all lesbians is part of what makes it possible for us to be so comfortable with each other. We know we can be our full selves here. We go hiking together. When someone says, "Hiking makes me think of partisans. This skill could be useful if we ever need to escape," no one thinks this is strange. We make outrageous jokes that we know we could never repeat to anyone outside this group. We have fun. This surprises some of us, who thought this whole weekend would be ultra-intense. We swim, eat, play Trivial Pursuits and Boggle. We talk about sex. We sit in a circle, pass the *yahrtzheit* candle around, say the names of our family members who died in the Holocaust. We cry. We celebrate the passion for life together.

Am I coming closer to some integration of Jewishness in my heart, journeying beyond reading stacks of library books? Will I find a home in spiritual Judaism? Or will I feel alienated from this also, from the warmth of singing and ritual?

HOLDING THE TORAH

Lori is studying to be a rabbi. I am partners with this passionate, gentle woman of integrity who was thrilled because at the Jewish Renewal center *Elat Chayyim*, where she studied last summer, she got to pray for a whole week.

I never believed in God as a child, and now I am lovers with a rabbi-to-be. My lover is complex. She's a criminal defense lawyer. She also is an anti-racist, feminist, and gay rights activist. But spirituality is a growing part of her life. I tease her when we go to the Jewish bookstore because she goes immediately to the section I consider the scariest, the one with imposing leather-bound Talmudic texts, midrash commentary, while I lose myself in the fiction and history sections.

I held a Torah for the first time in my arms at Yom Kippur services last year. It was a little, portable Torah. We stood in a circle, men, women and a few small children, and passed it around. Some people held the Torah like a baby, rocking it to and fro, with looks of tenderness on their faces. Others touched the Torah with the fringes of their *tallitot* and then kissed the fringes.

The Torah scroll was passed to me. I stood there, holding it, in a state of extreme emotion. How many years had it been since someone in my family, almost certainly a man, had held a Torah? The Torah felt electric in my hand. It was all I could do not to drop it. Yet I wanted to hang onto it, to curl up with it and cry.

Lori and I went to Shabbat services at a house of one of the members of our *havurah*. They brought another Torah scroll. It would have been enough for me to see the Torah carried around the room like a small child in the arms of a dark-haired, tall woman. It would have been enough to kiss that child. It would have been enough to see the Torah undressed like a child, the velvet cover removed, the scroll unrolled, the ancient lettering on old parchment. It would have been enough to hear someone read a passage from that ancient scroll. But this Torah was a refugee, brought over from Germany two days before Kristallnacht. Two days before Kristallnacht a couple was leaving Germany for America. The rabbi at the local synagogue came to them and said, "I know you are not so religious, but these times are bad and we don't know what will come next. Will you take one of these Torah scrolls from the synagogue and bring it to America?" So this Torah scroll, like a treasured child, was carried to America in the arms of these two Jews. Two days later that synagogue was burnt to the ground and all the other Torah scrolls were destroyed.

I was looking at that Torah scroll, unveiled in a house in the mountains, on a rainy day in the redwoods. Lori was standing next to me holding my hand and I began to cry. I fled into the hallway, to stand under a painting by Sister Corita, Sister of Immaculate Heart of Mary, ironically enough the most famous Sister of the order of nuns who ran my Catholic high school. I stood under those colorful paintings and I wept. Lori came out into the hallway and comforted me and I held on to her as if all of the past was an ocean under my feet, sweeping me towards Germany.

Lori gave me the Hebrew necklace I wear everyday. On this necklace is my Hebrew name, the one I am taking, shyly growing into, the name Rina, which means Joyous Song. I have no Hebrew name from birth. Lori said I could have one, deserved one.

We went to visit my mother. I was getting dressed one morning. I got to the necklace, which I wear next to my collarbone. I just stood there, half-dressed, staring at Lori, saying, "Oh no. My mother will see this necklace if I wear this shirt. Should I wear it?" I decided to wear the necklace because I didn't want any more secrets. I put the silver necklace with the Hebrew letters around my neck and Lori went off to take a shower. My mother came into the room to talk to me, but she did not say anything about the necklace. Did she not notice the Hebrew letters? Did she notice them and decide not to say anything?

Later we were in a bookstore and a woman came up to me and asked what my necklace said. "I'm Jewish and can read a little Hebrew but can't quite make out the letters, sorry." "Rina," I said. I couldn't believe anybody was apologizing to *me* for not knowing better Hebrew. I felt like an impostor again.

Then Lori, my mother, and I walked along the river path. Lori was moving in the sun in front of me, the light soft on her tawny skin, her loose T-shirt slipping over one smooth muscular shoulder, sexy. I smiled at her and we kissed when my parents had their backs turned. She teased me for being a city slicker in my butch, pin-striped vest.

Then my mother announced, "I have a question for you, Lori. Do the Jewish people believe in the afterlife?" Lori hid her sadness well. She explained with her gentle clarity the differences on this question between most Reform Jews, and Jews who study Kabbalah. My mother said she did not know what the Kaddish was. She kept asking questions and listening to Lori's answers as if she were an anthropologist, as if she had absolutely no personal connection with Judaism.

I walked behind Lori, my feet catching on the asphalt, my heart unraveling in the aching light of the California day. Here was my mother, this woman who survived Kristallnacht and Nazi Germany, now seventy, my mother who raised me to not even know I was Jewish, here was my mother asking my Jewish lover if Jews believe in an afterlife. Why was she asking this question? Was she thinking about her own death? Was she simply intellectually curious? Or had someone visited her in dreams? I wanted to kiss Lori for the exquisite gentleness and respect with which she answered my mother, for the way she immediately sensed her vulnerability.

Several years after beginning to attend Jewish Renewal Shabbat services, my relationship to Jewish spirituality has altered to the point that I am no longer so afraid. I am now "practicing" Judaism. I am committing the final rebellion against my parents' assimilation. I am undeniably Jewish. It is not just something in my head, but sings through my heart and belly, dances in my feet.

My Jewish *chevre*, *Chadeish Yameinu*, has performed a kind of alchemy. Gradually my comfort level with Jewish spiritual practice has increased and sometimes I almost don't recognize this red-headed woman who rises to dance with a tambourine, who sings Hebrew prayers in the shower, who listens to Hebrew music in the car. I have hosted a Shabbat in my house, and felt the living room transformed by the Sh'ma prayer resonating through the walls.

"So have you lost it?" Lori asked.

"Lost what?"

"Your spiritual virginity?"

I laughed. "Oh yeah, I guess so." I laughed, but I felt incredibly vulnerable.

I think this is an apt description, because I do feel as if some big transformation is happening to me. It's like the difference between making love to a woman, and speaking abstractly of "loving women." I remember the first time I made love with a woman thinking, "Now I've really done it."

"I want you to feel this," Lori wrote to me once, "to feel the divine in your body. To find your way to ecstasy, to find that place where prayer and song and dance lead to ecstasy. Perhaps you have felt this in poetry or nature or making love? I want to share this with you, to show myself to you when I am moved this way."

Shall I tell her how I want to make love to granite, how I dream of lowering my body onto the warm flanks of stone, the icy flecks of quartz catching the light? How I dream the rock liquid again, rising, pushing into batholiths of stone, and then seized by fierce fingers of ice. Shall I tell her of the ecstasy of writing, how words rush through me like breath, *ruach*?

Maybe this geologic vision is the divine, my spirituality? In the past couple of years Jewish Renewal has become dear to me. But I want my mother's mountaintop, to fling my body into Jewish identity, including spirituality, like my mother flung her body onto the pine needle-covered earth on those southern California mountains of my childhood.

We went to a Shavuot retreat organized by the Renewal groups *Ruach Ha'aretz* (Spirit of the Earth) and the Aquarian Minyan. Shavuot is the holiday which commemorates the receiving of the Torah on Mount Sinai in the desert. It is traditional to stay up all night on Shavuot, singing and meditating and studying.

Lori and I brought our sleeping bags and pillows, and set them up in the center of a circle of chairs in the room where this all-night retreat was to take place. There were fifty strangers in the room with us. I was feeling shy, and anxious about what was about to transpire. I clung to Lori and felt critical of myself for this. We settled down in our nest of pillows as the singing began. It was only 9:30 p.m. and I was already exhausted, wondering how I was going to stay awake all night.

As song filled the room, I lay back on my sleeping bag, trying to avoid the hard, cold linoleum floor. Currents of music washed over me. I felt cradled, held in this circle of

Jewish people, healed and accepted. I cried a little, and Lori noticed and took my hand, looked tenderly at me.

All night we sang and studied and prayed. The idea, Rabbi Leah Novick explained later, is similar to a vision quest, to put people into an altered state, so that by dawn we were ready for the revelations of Torah. Rabbi Yitzak Marmorstein from Vancouver shared with us the teachings of Rav Kook, a rabbi and philosopher, one of the greatest Jewish thinkers of the past hundred years. "Torah is in us," he said. "We are God."

"Each of us has our own torah, our own life story which we both learn and teach from, said Rabbi Victor Gross. "And so many Jews in Jewish Renewal re-enter Judaism through doors of pain, the torah of pain." Is this my torah, I wondered, the torah of assimilation, the Holocaust, exile? Rabbi Gross went on, "Each of us is born on this earth to write their own torah."

The next day I sat in a redwood-encircled amphitheater and felt his words nestle deep in my chest. If I have a torah to write, it must be this torah, this story of my family during the *Shoah*, this memoir. This torah is written with fire, with the words that are the legacy from my family. This torah is written in tears. This torah is written in love.

They say the Torah is written in black fire on white fire. Black fire is the letters; white fire is space between. If this white fire is the space between the letters, does white fire represent silence, what has not been said? If so, then my torah is white fire transmuting into black fire, containing both silence and words.

Over the past few years Lori and I have honored Shabbat in a number of landscapes: on a tiny beach in Jamaica as the iridescent waters of the Caribbean rolled in and out; in a snow-covered meadow in the High Sierra, where I watched the brilliant mountain light bounce off the soft bellies of snowdrifts, by the Russian River in Guerneville, California. I am learning to sing and pray outside, to feel my body both as part of the landscape and as a conduit for prayer. "Remember that on Sinai we were outside in nature and were purified," Rabbi Leah Novick said in the middle of the night of Shavuot, and I thought of my mother's mountaintop.

Are these snowdrifts, these fir and pine and redwood trees, these granite boulders, these coral reefs, these tropical flowers and birds, these rivers, and these hands—is all this *Yah, Ruach, Shekhinah*, dare I say it: God?

They say Hebrew letters are sacred containers of light. If letters and language are sacred conduits, then language is a sacred path. I walk this path of *Zakhor*, speaking this sacred story.

The days after I returned from Shavuot were intense, filled with dreams only half-remembered. I woke myself up murmuring, crying. Three days after I returned, my mother called me. "I thought you'd want to know my sister went to Nuremberg," she told me. "She was interviewed by a museum there about her life as a child. I think they are interviewing other people who left Nuremberg too; they even went all the way to New York to interview some people."

I was struck by two things: one, that my mother had initiated a conversation with me about the Holocaust, and two, that she never mentioned the word *Holocaust*, *Nazi*, or *Jew*.

"She was interviewed for an hour," my mother said, "She said she was really sweating it because the interview was in German and she was struggling to remember her German. Finally they told her it was fine to say it in English. But I don't know how she talked for an hour. If you interviewed me I would only be able to talk for five minutes because I don't remember anything." She laughed. I held the phone away from my mouth, afraid she would hear me taking in a deep, painful breath.

"There's a website about Nuremberg," I told her. "It has a list of all the Jews from there who died in the Holocaust. Some of them have our family name. They must be related to us."

"I doubt it," she said. "My father's three sisters all married and my uncle's name was Sondhelm. He committed suicide when the war started."

"But maybe the museum that put that list together, maybe that's the same museum that interviewed your sister?" I mused.

"Maybe," my mother replied. "What's the address for that site?"

I was amazed that my mother was actually considering looking at this website. She went on talking.

"Eva also met with her childhood classmates. They had all sorts of presents for her. One of them embroidered a whole tablecloth. Another remembered going to play at our parents' house. She remembered stuff that even Eva can't recall."

"Maybe that's because you had that amazing room full of toys."

"What room? My father ran a toy train factory."

"Yeah, but he got toys at trade shows. Eva told me you and she shared a room so that you could use the other room as a playroom."

"Oh, see I have no memories of that," my mother confessed.

I was silent, trying to imagine not remembering my childhood room. But I was also happy to be able to tell my mother a sweet story about the childhood she does not remember.

Was this ten-minute conversation a tiny easing of silence, a beginning of some kind of dialogue between my mother and me about the Holocaust? When I cast myself as the wicked daughter, re-exposing my mother to trauma through my writing, am I wrong? One generation after the *Shoah*, I have been given the gifts of being able to look this catastrophe in the face, to trace its path deep into the emotional history of my family. Through my writing, something becomes whole again.

In July, 1999 Lori and I drove north to Corvallis, Oregon to attend the Kallah, the biannual Jewish Renewal gathering. Over 750 Jews of all ages and diverse backgrounds came together on a tree-shaded college campus. I was swept into an intense wave of praying, singing, dancing, studying, and conversing, which began at 7 a.m. each morning and lasted until past midnight. I started my day with Jewish Yoga or a running minyan. I studied for a week with Rabbi Naomi Steinberg, whose work on behalf of saving the old-growth redwoods in northern California has inspired people across the country. I also studied with Rabbi Elliot Ginsburg, a powerful teacher of Kabbalah. In one incredible afternoon I joined fofty four women in an outdoor mikvah, in which I swam in a lake almost without fear for the first time, and performed a ritual immersion to try to rid myself of anxiety.

But it was Tisha b'Av which possessed me, Tisha b'Av, which transformed me. Tisha b'Av, the 9th day of the month of *Av* on the Jewish calendar, is a haunting day in Jewish history and tradition. On this day both the first and second Temples were destroyed in Jerusalem, sending us into exile. On this day, Jews were expelled from England, and from Spain in 1492.

Traditionally Tisha b'Av is observed as a fast day, a day of mourning. We sit on the ground. We do not wear leather. We wear old clothes and do not make love. We feel ourselves as refugees from history. We experience Jewish exile in our bones, all the great expulsions of our people. We allow ourselves to be broken-hearted, in grief. For only by fully releasing this grief can we release ourselves into life. As Rabbi Marsha Prager said at a panel at the Kallah, "We seek the treasure of God in the ruin of the human heart."

The Kallah began on a Sunday and seemed to build inevitably towards Tisha b'Av, which was on a Thursday. At first, I found myself resistant to this day of mourning. Here I was at the Kallah, surrounded by dynamic and fascinating Jews of all persuasions. Why should I contract, grieve, withdraw? I am a child of refugees. Hadn't I spent enough of my life mourning Jewish exile? But my teachers showed me that this day is a gift, an enclosed space in which I could fully grieve and rage against history, not alone, but in community. Tisha B'Av is a day of opening, of moving through feelings, being broken-hearted, but then letting go, opening to the joy of Shabbat which will follow the next day.

I fasted, allowing myself to feel empty. I did not take the world into my body. I lay under a tree at noon and melted into the light glistening on the maple leaves above my head. "Exile equals empty," I wrote in my journal. "Refugee. Refuge. Refuse." I felt my family as refuse, tossed across the world. A train passed on the tracks a few yards from where I sprawled. "Train of death," I wrote. "Train of leaving. No food in my belly, only the vibrations of this train. My mother's broken heart in the land of death trains. I want to hold her close." After I wrote this I lay under the tree for awhile and thought about my mother and cried. Then I felt better.

I went to my afternoon class with Rabbi Elliot Ginsburg. He had asked us to bring a scarf or *tallit* to wrap ourselves in. The evening before I had gotten myself my first *tallit* at the Kallah bookstore, a stunning silk prayer shawl with a tree of life painted on it, a tree with golden limbs and purple and green leaves. Was it okay to get myself this present? Some of the old insecurities surfaced. Was I Jewish enough to have a *tallit*? Did I deserve one? I sighed, decided to disregard these voices and give myself this gift.

I arrived at class carrying my new *tallit*. Elliot divided us up into groups of three. He told us we were going to be each other's angels. One of my angels was another daughter of survivors whom I knew from a small group I was facilitating at the Kallah for children of Holocaust survivors.

We went outside carrying folding chairs. We chose one chair as the life chair, and one chair as the death chair. Our task was to connect with two moments: a moment of brokenness, when something was dying in us and a moment of life, when something was being born in us.

I went first. I sat in the death chair. My two angels stood at each end of the chairs, holding the energy over me like a Jewish wedding canopy, a *chuppah*. I wrapped myself in my silken *tallit* and told the story of death, of my family's exile, amnesia, how it was passed on to me in the form of shadows and silence. I was quiet a moment, wrapped in my *tallit*. I listened to the sound of the leaves in the wind, to the murmuring voices in other chairs beyond our enchanted circle.

Then I got up and moved to the life chair. My voice grew stronger as I said: "I am the woman who has chosen to be Jewish, despite this history of terror and exile. I am the woman who is learning how to sing and pray, to dance with tambourines. I am the woman who is wearing this *tallit* for the first time, this *tallit* of winged light, painted with the Tree of Life, which symbolizes my love of nature, and my belief in hope despite the broken tree of my family, the broken Jewish trees of the Holocaust. I am the part of me who loves myself Jewish, who loves myself."

Under this *chuppah* I married my Jewishness, my deepest self. I sat silently a few moments, feeling the emptiness, the broken-heartedness ebb. Then I rose to be held by my angels, who hugged me and cried with me, then marked their own life passages, while I became the angel for them.

After Tisha b'Av I finally understood the interweaving of suffering and joy in Jewish history, in Judaism, the long path of exile and ecstasy that brought me to this moment—to be the keeper of memory.

BIBLIOGRAPHY

Encyclopedia Judaica. Jerusalem: Keter Publishing House, 1996.

Epstein, Helen. *Children of the Holocaust*. New York: Putnam, 1979.

Gershon, Karen, ed. *We Came As Children: A Collective Autobiography*. New York: Harcourt, Brace, and World, 1966.

Holthaus, Gary. *In the Thoreau Tradition*, conference in Missoula, Montana, 1995.

Kaplan, Marion A. *Between Dignity and Despair: Jewish Life in Nazi Germany*. New York: Oxford University Press, 1998.

Kestenberg, J.S. and Brenner, Ira. *The Last Witness: The Child Survivor of the Holocaust*. Washington, D.C.: American Psychiatric Press, 1996.

Lorde, Audre. "The Transformation of Silence Into Language and Action," in *Sister Outsider*. Freedom, California: The Crossing Press, 1984.

Rubin, Barry. *Assimilation and its Discontents*. New York: Random House, 1995.

Swartz, Sarah Silberstein and Margie Wolfe, eds. *From Memory to Transformation: Jewish Women's Voices*. Toronto: Second Story Press, 1998.

ABOUT THE AUTHOR:

Irene Reti's writing has been published in *Ghosts of the Holocaust: An Anthology of Poetry by the Second Generation, Word of Mouth II, The Hedgebrook News,* and other publications. She is the co-editor of *Women Runners: Stories of Transformation* (Breakaway Books 2001), and *A Transported Life: Memories of Kindertransport, the Oral History of Thea Feliks Eden* (HerBooks 1995). Reti has been a writer-in-residence at Hedgebrook and Norcroft writing colonies. She works as an editor/oral historian for the Regional History Project at the University of California, Santa Cruz.

HERBOOKS TITLES
P. O. BOX 7467
SANTA CRUZ, CA 95061
http://members.cruzio.com/~herbooks/

Mail orders welcome. **Individuals:** Please include $3.00 postage for the first book; 25 for each additional book or order from your favorite bookstore. **Bookstores:** *The Keeper of Memory* may be ordered from the Ingram Book Company 1-800-937-8000 or direct from HerBooks. Other titles may be ordered from Alamo Square Distributors or direct from HerBooks.

The Keeper of Memory: A Memoir by Irene Reti / $12.95
The Second Coming of Joan of Arc and other Plays by Carolyn Gage/ $10.00
A Transported Life: Memories of Kindertransport, The Oral History of Thea Feliks Eden, edited by Irene Reti and Valerie Jean Chase / $9.00
Garden Variety Dykes: Lesbian Traditions in Gardening edited by Irene Reti and Valerie Jean Chase/ $10.00
Unleashing Feminism: critiquing Lesbian Sadomasochism in the Gay Nineties a collection of Radical Feminist Writings edited by Irene Reti / $8.95
Love, Politics and "Rescue" in Lesbian Relationships an essay by Diana Rabenold/ $3.50
Lizards/Los Padres stories by Bettianne Shoney Sien / $7.00
To Live with the Weeds poems by D.A. Clarke / $7.00
messages: music for lesbians cassette D.A. Clarke / $6.00